BATTLE

— OF —

WHISKEY VALLEY

By

ERMAN SANDS

Cover and Interior design by:
Miguel S. Kilantang, Jr.
www.migzworks.com

ISBN-13: 978-1497559424
ISBN-10: 1497559421

Contents

DEDICATION

This book is dedicated to my wife, a loving family and friends both near and far, who give unbelievable support to my writing efforts.

CHAPTER 1

He came out of the woods into the road. His dark form created a stark contrast to the sunlit white Dogwood blossoms. Waldo Wickers stepped into the road and waved both hands franticly to stop the noisy old car.

"Looks like Waldo Wickers the third." The tall skinny Gil pumped on the brake petal. It took him a little time to work up enough resistance to stop the car.

"Now there's a feller I haven't figured out yet. Why did he move way up here in the mountains? He has done his best to bring the city with him." The younger, broader Milton shifted the loaded .30-.30

Winchester to the other side of his knee.

Waldo scurried up to the driver's door. "My truck is down the road a little way. Can I have a ride down to it?"

Waldo twisted on the back door handle before Gil had time to answer.

"Howdee Waldo." Milton spoke sarcastically, his face grew dark. "What's got you in such a dither you can't say hello to a couple of good old boys?"

"I found a whiskey still and I have to get to town so I can report it."

Gil and Milton looked at each other.

"Are you sure it was a whiskey still?" Gil asked.

"I sure am. The still is set up beside the big spring on the forks of Lion Creek."

"Some of them metal things they put out to salt cows in look like a still." Milton ventured.

"This was no salt ground!" Waldo was excited and adamant. "There's a fifty-five gallon barrel of moonshine there. I know its moonshine. I got me a drink of it. I'm going to call the Revenue Service."

"The closest telephone is in town. That's fifty

miles of rough road." Gil watched Waldo in the mirror.

"It's kind of rough to drink a man's whiskey and turn him in for making it." Milton tried one last time.

Gil glanced at Milton and gave an almost imperceptible shake of his head. Milton turned to face straight ahead. His grip on the rifle barrel tightened. They rode on in silence.

"My truck is just down this little side road. I'll get off here."

Both men silently watched Waldo stride away oblivious to the warm sun or the beautiful early spring flowers scattered alongside the road. He was so busy reaching in his pocket for the keys he failed to notice the yellowish green tint the new leaves cast over the low mountains.

"I'll take back what I said awhile ago. I have figured that feller out." Milton turned his head to watch Waldo disappear. "He don't want to live in the hills does he?"

"He wants to bring the city with him. If he was

smart he'd take his clothes to town with him." Gil shook his head. "You know I don't drink a drop. But to go turn a neighbor, what ain't done nothing to him, in to the Revenoors. That's sinking mighty low."

"He better go kiss that new barn he built and filled with all that high dollar feed."

Gil shook his head. "It won't make much difference if the barn and that feed do burn. He won't have anything to feed it to. I can see all them fancy Herefords he brought in here are mighty sick. It looks like arsenic fever to me."

"It's too bad. He don't really seem to be too bad a guy except he can't mind his own business." Milton was silent for awhile. "He asked me how to get along here in the valley when he first bought the Harky place. I told him to be a good neighbor. I don't think he can hear very well."

Gil shifted down a gear to slow the car down to meet three horsemen. The horsemen lined up on the same side of the road. Gil pumped the brakes hard and fast the old rig managed to stop in the vicinity of the horsemen.

The first horseman was riding with a hundred pounds of sugar across his lap. The other two horsemen had a sack of corn across their saddle. The first horseman moved close to the door. "Howdy Gil." Placing both hands on the sugar he leaned over far enough to see Milton. "You aren't particular who you run around with are you?"

"He's talking to you ain't he Pots?" Milton smiled

Pots shifted the lump of tobacco in his jaw, tracked a bug crawling across the dusty road and let go, he expertly speared the hapless insect with a stream of tobacco juice. "At least you fellows will say good morning. We just met that Mister Waldo Wickers the third. Not only did he not say hello, he didn't even wave. In fact he didn't even slow down. He left us peons eating his dust."

Gil sat thoughtful for a minute then made up his mind. "Old Waldo's been to Buck Horn Springs at the fork of Lion Creek. Now he's in a hurry to get to town."

Pots turned to look at the other two horsemen

who'd remained silent except to wave. Pots' face turned red and his eyes hardened. He turned back to the window. "I'd love to stay and chew the rag with you all but we have got work that needs to be done. Thank you. You all come see us, you hear?" In spite of the heavy loads Pot's group left at a trot.

"Well them boys don't have to worry about the Sheriff anyway." Milton watched the horses until they were out of sight.

"Jim Skaggs will not come up in this valley. He knows some of these boys don't like him too well." Gil maneuvered around a big rock in the road. "I haven't seen a Sheriff in the valley unless its election time or somebody gets killed. Then it takes him three or four days to get up here. He waits for everyone to sober up and the shooting to stop."

"Pots loves those elections. The Sheriff buys moonshine from him by the keg. Jim gives us a drink of shine and asks us to vote for him. I know you don't drink but I never can make up my mind as to who I'm going to vote for at election time. That way I get several drinks from all the candidates." Milton chuckled.

"We don't need or want the Sheriff up here. The people moved up in the hills to be left alone. If there is trouble they will settle it among themselves. Why if that Sheriff made it a habit of coming up here we'd have to have a drivers license and buy license tags for these old cars."

The battered old Ford rattled along. Steam came from the radiator and a cloud of smoke bellowed from the exhaust. An oil fouled spark plug had one cylinder misfiring on a regular basis but the old cripple weaved its treadless tires through the rocks at a steady twenty-five miles an hour. The men carried on a desultory conversation for the next mile or so until Milton said, "stop!"

Gil wrestled the old car to a stop, "what is it?" Gil noticed Milt hadn't moved the rifle so he knew it wasn't a deer.

"I don't know but I thought I saw a flash of light off a windshield. It might be a Game Warden looking for us." Milt turned in the seat so he could stare into the trees as the car rolled backward. "Whoa!

Yeah, there it is. It's a pickup all right. I can't quite make her out. Back a little farther. There it is. See beside that big Yellow Pine. Look just over the top of the little Black Gum."

"Yeah I see it but I can't make it out. Does it look like Dan's truck?"

"Can't tell. Hold on and I'll see." Milt stepped out the door with the rifle in his hand. Gil sat patiently waiting with the engine idling.

Milt jumped the ditch and reached for the door handle. "It's the pickup Dave Miloy has been driving. It looks like he went up Bean Creek. At least he was going that way when he left the truck."

"He's looking for Pots and the Swann Brother's still. What's happened to this younger generation? Dan's a Game Warden and Dave's a stinking Revenue Agent." Gil eased the car on down the dusty lane.

"It's them fancy colleges. I knew them two boys were ruined as soon as I heard they were going to go to one of them places. I told Missy them boys won't be fit to shoot inside of six months. It's worse than

I thought. They came back to harass the people they grew up with." Milton pulled a sack of Country Gentleman tobacco from one pocket and a book of OCB cigarette papers from another.

"Yeah, I remember the first time I heard them college professors believe that man used to swing by his tail. They teach all kinds of crazy things. I'm sure glad none of my kids wanted to go to one them places. That place has turned Dan and Dave into sorry snots." Gil made a chopping motion with his hand.

"Now, I want you to stop and think about Dan for minute. Who has Dan arrested? He ain't bothered anyone from this valley yet. He hangs around that lake and gives them flatlanders a bad time but he's left the home folk alone. He's let us hunt and fish what we want, when we want. We may have a better deal with him than we'd have with an outsider,

"Dave is a different story. That boy is a traitor. He cut his teeth on kindling wood for the firebox of a whiskey still. His daddy used to operate the best still in the valley. Dave's daddy inherited that still from Dave's Grandpa. Now he's busting up stills and sending people to jail. He knows where and how to find them too. He even knows which clans to watch. And he knows which members of a clan are most likely to be making whiskey. Do you think his ancestors might have swung by their tails?"

Dave watched the silver stream of water slide down the green strands of moss and fall babbling into the cold clear pool below it. Small bubbles of white water boiled back to the surface. Sunlight reflected on the sides of the small bass who flashed out of his ambush to smack a hapless bug on the surface of the water. The trees maintained their brooding silence and cast a cool shade over the granite boulders. A soft breeze whispered its way through the treetops. The temperature was perfect. The warm sun caressed his shoulder blades. This made him want to lay on a rock to stretch, doze and dream. It was one of those ideal spring days. Here the world was at peace.

Bean Canyon rose in an array of small, gurgling

water falls and huge boulders covered by the cool calm shade. The peace, solitude and beauty of the place were lost on Dave.

Resting his lean five foot ten frame against a big red oak tree Dave removed the baseball cap and ran long fingers through the damp blond hair. His gray eyes wandered over the stream ahead then turned to roam over treetops back to the point where Bean Creek joined the river. Then he smelled it. The skunkish smell of a mad Cottonmouth permeated the clean mountain air. He paid close attention to the terrain around his feet. He searched thoroughly. His eye settled on a black fringe under a granite boulder. Stooping Dave looked under the rock. There he was. A big black snake rolled up in his fighting coil. When Dave's head leaned over far enough to see the snake it leaned its head back and opened its mouth. The snow white mouth and large fangs declared to the world he was a bad dude. Just stay out of striking distance and we'll get along.

Dave sidestepped the cottonmouth and leaped upon another granite boulder. He didn't have time to kill a cottonmouth. His frustration increased as he trudged on up Bean Creek. He watched for smoke. He tested the pristine air by smell. He checked the trails for tracks. Where could that whiskey still be located? At the head of the creek he found a log facing the canyon and settled back in the warm sun to recuperate from the long climb.

Six months ago the Director called Dave into his office. "There's a stream of moonshine whiskey crossing the Stateline. Harold and Chester have had no luck shutting the stills down or finding out how the whiskey is transported. We've assigned you to the third district. See if you can shut those stills down."

Dave hung his head in silent thought. This was one assignment he did not want. It was an assignment he promised himself he'd never take when he entered the Academy. There was no way he wanted to work among his own people.

"You see sir that is the country I grew up in. A lot of the people in those hills are relatives of mine. I know all the rest."

"Are you refusing the assignment?" The Director glared down the double barreled bore of the little lens perched on his nose.

This was serious. If he said yes Dave knew he'd be shipped to a nondescript station in Outer Siberia and forgotten. He'd serve there for twenty years or until he died of boredom. His career would be essentially over before it got started. What a predicament to be in on his first assignment. "No sir I'm not refusing. I'm just respectfully requesting another assignment. I know all those people and all those people know me. There would be no chance to find out anything before they knew I was a Revenue Agent."

"That is precisely why we're sending you in there. You know the people and the land. Perhaps some of your relatives or friends will help you out." The Director paused for breath and walked to the window. He stared pensively out the window and turned to Dave. "There is no way we can get an under cover agent in there. We tried the old pilgrim on a fishing vacation ploy. "Chester and Harold didn't have the camp set up half an hour when a ten year old boy rode by on a mule. Harold lured him into camp with the promise of a cold pop and tried to ask leading questions. The boy drank the pop walked to the boat and examined it admiringly then allowed as to how well the Government equipped Revenuer Agents when they sent them out to hunt stills.

"The lad hopped onto the mule and suggested the Agents look around the unusual rock at the edge of the campground and rode away. Chester strode over to the rock and picked up a pint of the best moonshine whiskey you ever saw.

"It's been frustrating. We've never gotten an undercover agent in those hills yet."

"Yes sir, I know." Dave laughed. "I've seen some of those efforts. It is a close nit community. A stranger can move in and twenty years later he's still that stranger from somewhere."

"How can it be done?" The Director fished around the subject. "We could kick you out of the agency."

"No sir!" Dave snapped fully alert. "I will not go in there like a Judas goat! I will quit first!"

"We've found that not only do all those people know each other, their fathers and their father's fathers knew each other. It is impossible to plant someone in there. Even the people who don't operate a still are against us. People who don't even drink are against us." The Director seated himself behind his desk. "They have no respect for the law."

"It's not just a lack of respect for the law. It's a total distrust of the law. To them the badge on a man's shirt means he's the lowest, lyingest, stealingest, bribe taking thief in the human race, hid behind a badge. They have more respect for a bank robber than they do for a judge. The bank robber is a thief but he doesn't claim to be anything else and takes his chances like anyone else. They feel a judge is a sanctimonious, cowardly thief and robber hiding behind the black robe of the law. These people have had nothing but bad contacts with the law. Nothing good has ever come to them from the law. This is why church going people who don't drink will protect the still operators.

"They don't need or want the law to protect them. They protect each other and themselves. They equate the law with a rattlesnake. Either will bite you if you give them a chance. You know as well as I do the stills that send the whiskey across the Stateline pay a bribe to the local Sheriff. You realize if you plant someone in there and the people find out who they are you will have a dead agent on your hands, be they man or woman."

"A woman? A woman?" The Director leaned forward and steeped his fingers. "You may have something there. Pick up your transfer orders at the front desk on your way out."

Dave was in turmoil. He left the Director's office and strolled slowly down the hall. This was the hardest decision he'd had to make in all his twenty-six years of living on this earth. If he refused the assignment he'd be ahead to just turn his badge in. He'd worked so hard to get here. It was the answer to a dream. If he refused the assignment it was over today. If he accepted, it would give him time to work out something.

He rubbed those memories from his eyes with the back of his hand and thought of Vera Lee. A lot of time passed since he'd seen her. They were a thing during their senior year. There was gossip around that they were going to wed. She was upset when he told her he passed the entrance exam to State College and even more upset when she learned he was going into law enforcement. She was furious when she learned he had his eyes set on becoming a "Revoonor".

She wasn't married yet. By now everyone in the valley knew he was back. No use skirting the byways anymore. Yep, he thought I'll come out in the open. He rose and started the long walk back to his truck. He wondered what Vera Lee looked like now. Had she changed?

How much had he changed?

Dense forests of big Oak trees lined the country lane. A setting sun flickered sunbeams across the road between the trunks of the huge trees. A soft little breeze carried away the dust he fogged up behind him. He felt much better. He wouldn't admit it to himself but the thought of seeing Vera Lee cheered him up. Perhaps they could find some sort of common ground. Splashing across a small creek and round a corner he brought the truck to a halt in front of an open gate in the white picket fence.

He switched the key off as he took in the sights. The white two story house was tucked away under a brace of three hundred year old Red Oaks. Clucking steadily a hen led a brood of fuzzy yellow chicks along the yard fence in search of bugs. He could hear a litter of pigs jockey for a place at the dinner table. Mom grunted her satisfaction as the pigs nursed. A rooster flapped his wings and crowed behind the house. Tranquility he thought. It was something he'd not learned to appreciate until he went to the Academy. It is one of those things a person never appreciates until he has lost it.

The place really had not changed much. There was a new picket fence around the yard and the barn had been painted a different color. He glanced at the upstairs window he knew to be Vera Lee's room.

An arthritic old hound came out to bay at him.

Dave opened the door and dropped to one knee. "What's the matter Dan? Don't you remember me?" The old dog looked puzzled then the light of recognition entered his eyes and wagging his tail he shuffled to Dave. "You remember me. We used to chase those foxes together." Dave took the old dog's head in both hands and scratched the secret spots behind his ears.

"What are you doing with my dog?" The coarse voice lashed at Dave. Dave looked up to see Jason Marley's red face over the gate in the picket fence. "I don't think he's made much whiskey today. You can turn him loose."

Dave looked up. "Hello, Mr. Marley I ..."

"We don't inform on the neighbors. No need for you to waste your time."

"Mr. Marley I'd never ask you to..."

"No? Well you'd hang around hoping some of us would slip up and give you some information?" Marley stepped through the gate with his hands on his hip.

CHAPTER 2

Dave looked at him and caught a movement in the upstairs window over Marley's head. A hand drew the curtains aside and a pale face appeared behind the sash.

"Mr. Marly I ..."

"If you've come to see Vera Lee forget it! She wants nothing to do with you." Marley crowded him.

When Dave turned to his truck he saw a hand make a feeble wave beside the face in the upstairs window. Leaping into the truck Dave threw dirt around the turn. He slammed through the creek. Water flew everywhere. The engine missed ominously when the water splashed onto the ignition system. He blew dust up in great clouds on his way to the county road. By the time he reached the county road his anger had settled into the chill of depression.

What was he doing here anyway? Perhaps it was better that both his parents were gone. At least they didn't have to see what their son had come to. Perhaps he should walk into the office and throw his badge at the Director. They should not have sent him back here. It was totally unfair to be sent back here! He did not want this!

Vera Lee sat in front of the mirror and arranged her hair. Then she rearranged it again. She was restless. She always knew Dave would come back. When Jack barked and she looked out the window her heart did a flip flop. He was back! She was about to rush out when she saw her father approach the gate.

Her excitement died down and she realized Dave was driving an Agency truck and had a badge pinned on his chest. Why did he have to do this? How could he be so stubborn? Could he not see?

He was an outcast in the valley and if she married him she would be in the same boat. She was the Queen Bee in the valley. If she married him she would share in his fate. She could not do this.

Of all the nerve! She'd given him a choice and he'd taken the agency. Never in her wildest dream did she realize he would choose the agency. Once the words were out, her pride wouldn't let her take them back. Besides, she was sure he would come to his senses and realize what he lost and come apologetically back.

Why did he come back to the valley? She was sure he'd come back because she was here. Why else? His folks were dead and the land was all sold. He'd come partway back. She would stick to her guns and ignore him until he came to his senses and quit the agency. She was sure it would work. When he came back she would explain that her father had forbid her to speak to him.

Almost automatically Dave turned into Harper's Country Store. The store hadn't changed a particle. The same tin roof, the same board and bat siding.

The Coke Cola sign still hung crookedly over the door. The sign on the door informed the world RC and Orange Crush Soda were sold inside. Driving to the single gas pump Dave took the handle down and tried to pump gasoline into the overhead bowl. Nothing happened. He tried it several times. Nothing. Oh well, that thing had been cranky for years.

Harper sat in his usual place behind the counter. "I see that pump is still giving you trouble?" Dave asked.

"No trouble," Harper said curtly.

"It doesn't work." Dave was puzzled.

"It works. I turned it off and I'm out of anything else you need."

This stopped Dave in full stride toward the pop case. The fire of his anger, then the chill of the depression, and now this? The hammering in his temples tempered his resolve.

"Mr. Harper," Dave spun on his heel. "I don't like being here any better than anyone likes for me to be here. This is my chosen profession and I'll do a good job of it. You tell all these sanctimonious people to quit making moonshine and I'll be happy to leave.

"Now Mr. Harper, let's bring it closer to home. Either the ladies of this valley have made a lot of jelly or you supply sugar to the moonshiners. We both know it is the wrong season for jelly. I checked to see how much sugar you ordered before I came back. How many people buy sugar by the hundred pound sack? How many people have several sacks of sugar delivered to a stump or unusual rock on the side of the roadway? Payment for the sugar and a gallon of whiskey will be waiting there to be picked up by the delivery man.

I could have walked in here with a search warrant, pulled that box of books from behind your counter, the ones you use to keep track of the credit sales in. I would have the names of most of the people operateing stills. The manufacture and distribution of illegal whiskey is a felony and you have been aiding and abetting. If I'd come back in this frame of mind you would be in a lot of trouble.

"The stream of illegal booze across the river is

the reason I'm here. You can tell everyone to quit making whiskey and be mad at the person or persons who are trying to get rich. If they don't quit we will find the stills and when we do someone is going to spend time in the big house." Dave's glittering eyes softened a little. "I could take you in right now Mr. Harper. All I'd have to do is pull that jug of whiskey you have hid in the hollow stump at the back of the store."

"Who told you?" Mr. Harper was no longer indolent or insolent. Dave had his full attention.

"There you go again. Thinking someone turned you in." Dave's eyes softened even more and a smile curled his lips. "Mr. Harper you've had a jug hid in that stump for years. Us boys used to slip in and steal a drink. We were careful not to take enough that you would miss it."

It was Harper's turn to smile. "I'd forgotten you were one of those who did that. I knew you boys were getting into the whiskey but I didn't care as long as you didn't drink too much." The old man leaned back and relaxed. "As long as you thought you were stealing it none of you took too much. Boys steal whiskey today. It is a joy to watch them. They think they are so sneaky."

"You get rid of that jug because we're going to turn this country upside down and inside out until we stop the flow of bootleg whiskey across the river. If someone else finds the jug I might not be able to help you." Dave turned to the door. "The director is furious. The Governor told him he would send the National Guard in if we couldn't handle it. We will handle it."

"Dave," Dave stopped and turned. Mr. Harper crossed his arms on the counter. "Thank you. I still can't sell you anything. You know how these people are."

Dave shook his head and laughed, "Yeah, they're a hundred years behind time."

CHAPTER 3

Angry and disappointed Dave slammed through the door. A young lady attempted to step through the door at the same time. When he crashed into her his arms instinctively clasped her to his breast and he carried her a few steps forward trying to regain his balance. Dave turned red to his ears, released her and stepped back. "Mam I ..." He struggled for words.

With a big smile at his discomfort she extended her hand. "You must be the infamous David Miloy."

Dave was gaining his composure. "One and the same," he said and took the offered hand. Her handshake was firm like he expected a man's to be.

"Lesa Turner, I'm the school teacher. You don't seem to have four heads and I guess you dropped your pitchfork." She said playfully and smiled brilliantly.

"School Teacher? I bet you have heard some stories about me?"

"Yes, but I didn't expect you to sweep me off my feet the first time we met. I thought you'd clap iron on me and haul me off to some musty old Jail." There was something of a conspiratorial tone in these words Dave couldn't quite put a finger on. Lesa turned toward the door.

"I only put pretty girls in prison on the 5th Tuesday of each week." Dave moved toward his pickup.

Back in town Dave decided to call in his evening report before he went to eat. The nearest telephone was fifty dirt road miles from the valley. It really didn't make any difference though. The closest place he could get a room and a café meal was in town with the phone. He couldn't even buy a can of Spam and some crackers at Harper's store. The next store was twenty miles up the valley. He was sure his presence would be as welcome there as it had been at Harper's Store.

"Where have you been?" The director was excited. "We've been trying catch up with you."

"I've been tramping the woods looking for a whiskey still."

"We had an informant call in. Do you know where Buck Horn Springs are located? It is at the forks of Lion Creek. There is a large still there."

"Yes I know Buck Horn Springs well. I bet your informant was a fellow named Waldo Wickers." Dave thought back to this morning. "How did you know? Do you know this Waldo Wickers?"

"I saw him come out the mouth of Lion Creek and hitch a ride with Gil Sanders this morning. I don't know him well. He is a new comer to this part of the country." Dave mentally kicked himself. The signs were right there in front of him this morning.

"You should cultivate this Waldo guy. You might learn something you don't know." The director didn't know the hills or the folks that populated them.

"If Waldo told Gil he found that whiskey still, Waldo Wickers is about to learn a lesson. None of which will do him or us any good."

"I'll send Harold, Chester and some of the young guys who need experience out to you. You raid that still at daylight in the morning." The director didn't ask. He dictated.

"I'll go out tonight." Dave wasn't fond of the developing situation.

"You better wait for backup."

"I don't think I'll need it because I know the still will be gone. It will have been moved by now. I'm going tonight. You have Harold and Chester stand by. I'll call if I need them. As to those Academy boys you can keep them."

"Now you went on raids while you were in the Academy." The director was condescending.

"I went on flat ground. You keep them on flat ground. Up here a wrong move can touch off an unnecessary gun battle. You might lose some of them and more important you might lose me. I'm too young to die." Dave was hoping he could get across to the Director.

"You call back when you get out. The night clerk will be on duty and he can wake me if necessary." The director clicked off the line.

Dave held the phone for awhile and mentally kicked himself. Why do I have to antagonize the Director every time I talk to him? He asked himself.

Darkness swallowed the beam of his flashlight as Dave climbed Loin Creek. He was sure he'd find nothing at Buck Horn Springs so he wasn't even careful. He tromped along in a bad mood. He only hiked onto Lion Canyon because it was expected of him and he didn't want a large Revenue presence to stir up a strong resentment among the hill folks. They loved their freedom and a large raid would fire the flames of hatred among the decent people even more than among the bootleggers.

He didn't even notice the big round disk of a moon peek over Weaver's Knob. He failed to notice the ghostly shadows it created coming through the new foliage at the tops of the tall oaks. The shadows were playing hide and seek among the silent boulders. Dave grumbled on. He did not hear the symphony of the forest. Whippoorwills sang around him. Crickets, Cicada and a myriad of other insects threw their mating calls into the soft night air. Thousands of lightening bugs filled the air with flashing lights as they tried to attract a mate. A lonely Coyote sat on the mountainside and echoed his love songs from mountain to mountain. Dave kept the light on the ground looking for snakes.

The wobbling tremolo of a Screech Owl came in from the left. A gust of wind rustled the leaves. The bass hoot of a Great Horned Owl sifted through the trees. This jerked Dave back into the present and brought him to a complete stop. The hill folks communicated in the language of the great owl. They practiced it from childhood and could carry on limited conversations in owl talk. The only way anyone could tell the hillbilly from the real owl was to know the sound of his voice. Dave wondered if he could recognize any of the voices now.

The, "where are you?" call of the owl floated past him again.

"Here," the soft answer from the owl's mate came from behind Dave.

Dave stood and watched the moon push fingers of light across the sky. A big bird floated silently on the night air. He passed over Dave in the quest for his mate.

Dave decided he'd better wake up and put the hundred miles of rough dirt road and the hike up Lion Creek out of his mind. He knew the trip was worthless but he didn't want a task force rushing up the valley. He knew there would be no one at the springs but it was possible there would be and he sure didn't want to be the only one surprised. Moving ahead he proceeded with caution.

He walked into the springs, nothing there but some well tromped ground and a pile of ashes. He flicked the light around the area and swept it over the pile of ashes again. Something reflected the light. He slipped on a glove and carefully picked up a pint jar of moonshine whiskey left sitting on the pile of ashes. He smiled at the message the jar conveyed. What the shiners didn't take into consideration was that with today's technology the fingerprints on the jar would tie one or more of them to this jar of illegal whiskey and this abandoned still site.

There were three wood blocks, cut off trees, on either side of the fire. The moonshiners used them as seats. Did this mean there were three of them?

He sat on one of the blocks to rest and tried to feel which way the moonshiners went when they abandoned the site. A faint glow in the valley caught his attention. He sat watching it. It grew steadily larger until it revealed itself as a large structure fire. It was situated close to Waldo Wicker's place.

"Hey Waldo!" He shouted. "Welcome to the wonderful world of finking on moonshiners." Right then he settled down and swore to get this group. After looking the site over he knew several men were involved. He vowed to get them all. Up to now he'd been doing a job he didn't want to do. Now it was different. He wanted to nail their hides to the wall.

After they left Gil the moonshiners moved at a steady trot. Each wrapped in his private thoughts.

Pots thoughts were of revenge against Waldo. For cripes sake didn't Waldo know there wasn't a decent job in this valley. A man had to make a living somehow. Here in the valley you made it anyway you could. What was wrong with that city slicking piece of snot? What business was it of Waldo Wickers if they turned the ocean to whiskey? He would never see or be affected by any whiskey they made. None of them had molested Waldo in any manner, up until now anyway. It was time Waldo left this valley. They would show him the way out.

Pots and the Swann brothers weren't much worried about the Revenoors. It would take the Revenoors some time to react to the report. They would have to work hard and fast to move the still and it would slow their delivery down. They knew the Revenoors were hunting the still. They watched them search the hills on foot, on horses and in the air.

Normally the shiners would have hid the still and laid low until the Feds gave up. This buyer wanted a large amount of whiskey and he wanted it yesterday.

If they went into the delay mode they would lose the sale. This was the sixth time in so many weeks they'd moved the still. They were hoping to get all this order ran before the Revenoors forced them to move again.

Swinging out of the hardwoods along the creek Pots entered the large Yellow Pines and began climbing the point of a mountain. Three hundred yards from the trail he pulled up. Swinging out of the saddle he eased the sack of sugar to the ground.

"Do you boys think this is far enough from the trail?" Pots leaned over to look through the brush behind him.

Taking his lariat rope from the saddle he looped it around the bag, tossed the loose end over a limb and pulled the bag up. Satisfied it was going to work he lowered it to the ground. Fishing around in his possibles bag pulled out a handful of lard. He rubbed and greased a foot of the rope to keep the insects from coming down the rope then he hung the sugar high. The Swann brothers hung their burdens and the three headed for the still.

At the still they began expertly dismantling it. The thumper went on Pots saddle. The worm end-ed on Joe Joe Swann's Choctaw pony. They loaded various and sundry parts on Joe Jay Swann's horse.

"Hey Joe Jay," Pots stopped put his hands on his hips and looked at Joe Jay. "How come your Pappy named all of you guys with the same name? It shore makes it hard to tell you apart."

Joe Jay laughed. They had been through this many times before. "Pappy was half Choctaw and there were fourteen of us kids. He always said we were copies of him. His name was Joe so he named all fourteen of his kids Joe. This includes the girls. Is all this coming from a feller named Pots? Is that from your pot belly?"

Pots laughed easily. This banter could go on for hours, fill the time and mask the hard work they faced for the next few hours. "No, when I was small the sun used to shine on a cast-iron pot Mom heat-ed wash water in. The sun would warm the black pot. I used to crawl in there and cuddle up when it was cold. The name stuck. My real name is Albert

Rayett."

"*Al-bert Ra-y-ett?*" Joe Joe purposely mangled the name. "With a name like that it's no wonder you call yourself Pots. Where are we going with this thing anyway?"

"You say your Daddy was half Choctaw?"

"Yeah,"

"And your Mom was white?"

"Uhhuh, I'm one quarter Choctaw." Joe Joe was proud of his Indian heritage.

"Yeah, that is what I thought. You ain't nothing but a two bit Indian." Pots roared.

Joe Joe gave Pots a disparaging wave of the hand. "Where are we moving the still to? Where would be a good place?"

"I've been thinking about it. Let's set up at Skunk Springs on the head of Garland Creek. That place is like this one. It gives us several ways to run if we need it. What do you all think of that?"

"It's a long way to move but they'll tear these woods up looking for us." Joe Jay conceded.

"Ok with me, but let's went, I hear footprints

coming." Joe Joe led the horse across the stream. It was a tired group that returned after the second trip. "All we have left is that barrel of whiskey. Do you think we could leave it till morning? Be back up here about daybreak?" Joe Jay sat on one of the logs. "We'll to have to transfer that into five gallon cans to move it."

"Ordinarily I'd say yes but they sent Dave Miloy back here specifically to shut this still down. Dave is; smart, stubborn, knows the country and is a lot braver than those other candy puffs the Revenoors have sent. I'll bet you Dave will be here tonight." Joe Joe counted the reasons off on his fingers.

"I think you're right. And since old Dave will be out in the night air we'll leave him a pint of tonic. This will be just what he needs to warm the night chill out of his bones. Who knows he might get snake bit wandering around in the dark." They all laughed. Pots set a pint jar of whiskey on the pile of cold ashes.

They were climbing the mountain with the last of the whiskey when Joe Jay said "Whoa," softly. Everyone froze in place for a moment. Joe Jay pointed out the light in the canyon.

Quietly they passed on over the mountain. On the other side of the mountain Joe Joe pulled a handkerchief and wiped his brow. "That was cutting it too close."

"Old Dave was faster than I thought. If he comes upon us I'll whip him again. I used to whip him every other day when we were in school." Pots was imperturbable.

"I don't know," Joe Jay said. "If I remember right you never did manage to whip him."

"I beat him down so many times …"

"You did beat him down but you never whipped him. He always came back for more the next day. Him being after us kind of spooks me. What other Revenoor would have the nerve to be up here tonight?"

"None I guess. Do you fellows want to go by and say thank you to Waldo for a long days work?" Pots moved on.

"I'd rather gut shoot him." Joe Joe said sourly.

The trio tied their horses outside the fence and pulled saddle guns from boots on their saddles. "Now," Pots said. "I don't think Waldo will be laying for us but if he is shoot him. Don't mess around, shoot to kill."

"I don't think he will be laying for us because I don't think he knows how much trouble he is in. He could do this junk in the city and sleep comfortably. He ain't figured out he's not going to have another easy nights sleep in this valley."

They walked across the crisp stubble of the fresh mown meadow. Their crunching footsteps echoed off the dark bulk of the barn.

"Waldo built himself a nice barn didn't he?" Pots eyed the huge stack of hay the barn sheltered. "I can't see in the dark. Let's put a light in there so we can see what Waldo's hoarding up." Pots struck a match and pitched it on the hay.

The match smoked a moment then licked hungrily at the loose hay. Getting its start in the loose hay the flames took the first step up the stack of hay. The Swann Brothers walked around and set the barn afire all the way around. The light flickered over the tons of sacked feed stored in the other side of the barn.

Joe Jay tossed a sack of cow feed across his shoulders. Walking to the feed trough at the edge of the meadow he ripped the top out of the sack and poured the contents into the trough. He scattered the feed full length of the trough so the cows could all eat at the same time. Removing a bag of grayish white powder from his pocket he sprinkled it over the feed and then mixed it in.

At their horses Joe Joe turned to watch the growing flames. "It ought to take several days for that much hay to completely burn. We ought to be able to see fire and smoke for awhile."

CHAPTER 4

She was tall for a woman. Her slender body in the high necked, long sleeved, dress which ended well below her knees gave the illusion that she was taller than she really was. The auburn hair was pulled back into a severe bun and pinned at the nape of her neck. The crinkles around her soft gray eyes and smiling lips hinted at how much she enjoyed her job. Her slender fingers gripped the chalk that made scraping and screeching noises across the blackboard. She was in a hurry today.

"All right children." She tossed the chalk on the ledge. "That is your homework for the weekend. Be sure it is ready for Monday morning. This includes you Jeff. If you don't get better about doing your homework I'm going to have to speak to your father."

Jeff looked sheepishly at the teacher and shuffled the books in his large hands, "Aw Miss Turner, I'll try harder if you don't tell Pa. He gets awful mad." Jeff squeezed out of the small desk. He was the biggest boy in school. He stood taller than the teacher when he stood fully erect.

Lesa shook a finger at him. "See that you have that assignment completed and on my desk Monday morning! If you don't I'll have to tell Pots you flunked again. Ok children you have all did very well today so I'm going to let you go thirty minutes early."

Waving the children out of sight she walked around the school to the house provided by the school district. When she passed under the old pecan trees she pulled the pins from her hair, shook her head, and let the curls fall onto and around her shoulders.

Hurrying to the closet she donned a sheer low

cut white blouse, red skirt that ended well above her knees and a red jacket. Seating herself before the mirror she painted her lips a bright red. She patted powder over the rouge on her cheeks. Taking the perfume bottle she spread liberal puffs here and there.

From the next drawer she removed a jewelry box and hung a necklace around her throat, put two gaudy bracelets on her wrist and two beautiful rings on either hand.

When she rose and turned she was no longer Miss Lesa Turner the school marm. Her eyes were hard and the humor was gone from her face. She was now Lizzy Turner, a runner of bootleg booze. She hesitated until she'd run through a mental check list. She picked a set of keys from the dresser and a pair of red high heel shoes from the floor. She closed door gently. On her way to the small unused barn across the road she looked at the red shoes then the shoes she was wearing and shook her head. She couldn't don the red shoes until she got there. The heels might get in the way.

When she swung the barn door open a 1940 black Ford club coupe crouched in the semi-darkness. It was a little bit dirty. Not much, just about like a traveling car should be. All the dirt on this car was on the outside. The high compression engine under its hood was hopped up to the gills. The power tuned headers and twin exhaust were tucked under the hood. Twin pipes modestly turned down at rear of each front fender well. All the horsepower boosting equipment available had been added to the engine. The engine had taken some finessing to get. Through her track connections, she obtained it ten years before it went into public production. The transmission had been swiped from a four speed LaSalle. The tires were a grade heavier than usual. The suspension had been reworked to corner better at high speed and keep the car at the proper height and angle when loaded. The most special thing about this Ford was the tanks built into the body, fenders and floors. It could take on a hundred and twenty gallons of moonshine and look like Grandmother's car going to Sunday school.

She checked to make sure they filled the tanks properly. This was a Pots and Swann brother's load. The big engine kicked over, hesitated, and then answered with a roar. It galloped and sputtered while Lizzy closed the door. The big engine didn't like to idle. The beat picked up on the way to the main road. Once on the main road the sputter disappeared and the beat changed to the deep throated throb of a big powerful engine. The sounds reverberated off the school, the hills and small barn in a diminishingly smaller manner until all was quiet.

Lesa was an odd duck. She arrived in the valley to teach her first school. The first year everyone was leery and watchful. Her no nonsense way of teaching, generosity, common sense and courage led the people to totally adopt her. She was no longer "that Teacher".

It had been a year and a half since Louis stood on one foot then another, twisted his hands and asked her, "Miss Lesa would you go to the dance with me?"

Lesa thought it over. No one had invited her to

a dance before. They all assumed a teacher was too prim and proper to attend a dance. She knew some of the high and mighty would not like the teacher attending a dance. But what the heck, it was her life. Recreation had been very limited since she arrived. "I would love to go. What time do you want to pick me up?"

Louis couldn't believe what he'd just heard. "I, I." He stuttered. "Unless I can get hold of Billy Jack I'll have to leave the dance early." He'd been dreaming of this day and now he was going to miss part of it.

Lesa leaned back and watched his confusion with amused eyes. "Why will you leave early? Are you going to run a load of shine tonight?"

Louis's jaw dropped. "How did you know I was scheduled to make a run?" He demanded.

"I teach school, remember? You would be amazed at what the little birds tell me. Are you coming back tonight?"

Louis shook his head in the affirmative.

"Well, let's skip the dance and make the run."

Louis couldn't believe his ears again. "I ... I ... you ... you." He stuttered again. "You understand I'll be hauling a load of illegal whiskey."

"Yes."

"If I was to get caught and you were with me you'd be as guilty I was. It could mean time in the big house." Louis was trying to find a way out. "It could cost you your job."

"I know all that stuff."

"If we get jumped by the sheriff or feds I'd have to run for it. Do you think you can stand some fast driving?"

"My daddy built and raced cars. Up until his accident I rode fast cars. I not only can ride fast I can drive fast. I can also build a car that will run fast. I cut my teeth on a gear shift knob." Lesa was getting a little miffed at Louis's delay.

The run and delivery came off without any problem. They were back early enough for Lesa to get a couple hours of sleep. She couldn't sleep. The excitement and danger had her too keyed up to sleep. She had seen the money change hands. It made the pittance she received for teaching seem small indeed.

Lesa saved her money until she could afford to buy an old car. A couple of runs later she bought parts and began building the beauty she drove now.

Lizzy settled back and listened to the big engine throb. It was a thing you feel in your gut as well as hear with your ear. Since she finished the car Lizzy ran a majority of the whiskey that flowed from the valley. She followed her gut feelings. Sometime she'd stop when an officer gave chase. She could sit and charm him into feeling he was a cad for stopping such an alluring young lady or even suspicioning her of any wrong doing. Other times she turned the Olds engine loose to do its thing. The blistering acceleration and blazing straight away speed had always been enough.

The Olds engine was a thing of beauty. It had taken all the markers she had out, all her dad's markers and every ounce of persuasion she could muster to get her hands on one of the four engines. The engines were concept engines. General Motors manufactured many engines to use on test projects. Most were tossed into the furnaces and melted down. This particular model had shown so much promise GM scheduled it for the Oldsmobile several years in the future.

On a curvy road the Ford with its special suspension could out corner any of the stock cars the Revenoors used. The superior acceleration between corners let her disappear. She always had been right on which tactic to gamble on.

Her Dad began teaching her how to get the most out of an automobile at a young age. Since he had no sons his dream was to see Lesa become the first great woman driver on the track. Speed was very much a part of her early life.

Darkness settled like a warm blanket. Lizzy sat relaxed. The playful putter of the exhaust was music in her ears. Even though she strictly adhered to the speed limit she was going to be early.

She passed a dirt road and glanced up it from force of habit. She had to stay alert. The dim outline of the parked car gave its hiding place away. It was just a glimpse but it put her to watching the rear view mirror. The car came out and turned up the highway behind her without turning its lights on.

"Not today mister." She mumbled and put the petal to the metal. The Olds engine responded with an angry bellow and the Ford leaped away like a frightened gazelle. Headlights lit the highway behind her, then a flashing red-light and eventually a siren.

The Olds engine climbed from a roar to a high pitched whine. It sounded and felt healthy but the lights on the car behind her stayed at the same distance. She wasn't leaving them as fast as she should have. She checked the speedometer. It was climbing rapidly. It would soon hit the peg and be unable to register the true speed. Those lights behind her held their position.

The road was relative straight and the two cars hurtled through the night like run away rockets. Plunging down the hill Lizzy flashed across the river bridge. Stateline, this should stop the pursuit. The car behind her never slowed or faltered, it zipped across the bridge also. Holding the gas petal down with her left foot she put her right foot across the center hump and raked the shoe off it. When she brought her bare foot back across the transmission hump she rubbed it on the floor mat. She was going to need all the sensitivity she could manage in that foot.

"Feds!" Lizzy growled. "They have to be lousy Feds. Otherwise they would have stopped at the Stateline." Her mind raced. She catalogued the surrounding roads in her mind. "All right!" She yelled. "Let's see how you like to eat dirt and take corners."

Lizzy dropped a couple gears, braked hard and threw the back rapping flame throwing car onto a dirt road. Long flames flashed from the pipes on the deceleration then change to a steady glow when she stepped on the petal to break the back tires loose and toss the car into a skid around the corner. Her hand flew over and flipped a switch on the dashboard. The bellow of the Olds increased to a painful level of noise when the solenoids pulled the Lakes Plugs open and the engine began to breathe easier. Flames appeared behind each front wheel and the sound reflected off the fence posts. There was a definite frap tossed back off each telephone pole they shot past.

When Lizzy decided to haul shine she explored all the country roads along the routes she intended to use. She knew where she was going and what to expect when she got there. Great clouds of dust fogged up behind her. She turned the steering wheel left into the turn then frantically cranked it to the lock on the right. Her foot on the petal balanced the power to the back wheels. The spinning rear wheels balanced and matched the front wheels. A fast crank of the wheel to the left, a little off the gas then full on it again, and she came out of the slide at a high rate of speed. The digging spinning wheels threw up great clouds of dust. She tossed the Ford into another broadside around a sharp corner, looked into the mirror and smiled. There were no lights there. "Must be a city boy," she thought

"What the …?" She yelled. A set of headlights came through the dust inside her car on the turn!

She asked the big engine for every ounce of horsepower and RPM it contained and pulled away on the straight but lost most of the lead in the next corner. The fed was handling the dust very well.

"Ok. Ok. Keep yourself calm and go to plan B. What does he have in that car and who is driving it?" Shaking her head she turned back to the state highway.

Once on the highway again the cars smashed a roaring trail through the night. Exhaust pipes glowed as each engine stretched and strained for the one more horsepower that was going to make a difference in this battle.

Setting the car up very carefully Lizzy tapped the bar that was hooked into the emergency brake. When the back wheels broke loose she tossed the Ford into a 180 degree turn without leaving the pavement. She floored the petal in order to keep the rear tires spinning to brake her backward motion. She was still moving backward in a billowing cloud of rubber smoke when the Fed flashed past.

"That will be that!" She patted the Ford's dash.

Whoa! Those headlights hit her rearview mirror again. Where did the Feds get a driver who could drive like that and who built the car he was driving? She knew it had to be custom built. No factory ever built a car that could run with her Ford.

She tossed the car onto another dirt road and flashed past a sign that announced FROGVILLE 6. There were many ways in and out of Frogville but Lizzy planned to run a ten mile loop and come out where she went in. Meanwhile she had to, just had to, establish a little lead.

The thunderous roar of the flaming exhausts, high pitched scream of the engines and wail of the siren woke Granny Whooten from a sound sleep when they blasted past her bedroom windows.

"These darn kids now days." Granny sat up on her bed. "It's hard for a body to get a decent night sleep anymore." She climbed out of bed and dressed.

The chase continued to shatter the velvety quiet night air. Lizzy pushed the little Ford to its absolute maximum. She hoped the engine could stand these fire breathing entries, high revving turns and flat-out straight runs to the next curve. So far the little car met or exceeded every request. A pride rose in her breast. She built this car. She planned and torqued every bolt in the engine.

Who had built the black devil behind her? Where did the IRS get a car like that? The IRS usually ran cars acquired from the Highway Patrol. The little Ford could eat two of these for breakfast and never burp. Who was driving that black car? He not only matched her every move, he was doing it in the blinding dust storm she left in her wake. With the headlights reflecting off the dust into his eyes how could he judge and execute the high speed turns they were making? The possibility of failure raised its ugly head and surged through her.

Lizzy completed the loop and turned back toward Granny Whooten's house. She gained a little more lead on the pursuing car. She hoped it would be enough. What was that next curve? Left or right? How sharp was the bend? Was it flat? Did it go up-hill or down? Roll in or out. What was the road bed like on it? Was it dirt, gravel or deep dust? She flogged her brain for the information. She was exhausted. Her shoulders stung and her arms hurt. Exhausted people make mistakes. The first to make that mistake not only lost the race, they would most likely lose their life also. Sooner or later a tire had to blow. In these hard turns the tires rolled until the rocks battered the sidewalls. Sooner or later one of the rocks would puncture a sidewall and blow the tire. It would be head over teakettle time then. She thought of the roll bar she never put in the Ford to keep the weight down.

Granny Whooten opened the door of a dilapidated old truck parked facing the county road. When Lizzy flashed by she pulled the transmission of the old truck into neutral and stepped behind a big rock. The old truck rolled down the incline and bumped a hill of dirt on the other side of the road.

Sliding around the turn the Fed straightened up. His headlights picked up the old truck. It sat across the whole road from bank to drop off. Braking hard he tossed the car into a broad slide and stopped inches short of the old truck.

In the fog of dust Granny stepped from behind the rock and slammed the truck door. "What in tarnation are you doing?" She screamed.

Dave leaped from the car. "Move it! Move it!" He yelled.

"I can't move it. It won't start. I roll it down the hill to start it. When I saw you coming so durn fast it scared me. I didn't get it started before I got off the hill." Granny was working up a good mad. She walked toward Dave and shook an accusing finger at him. "You ought to be ashamed of yourself! Driving like that on a public road! I'm going to get the law on you!"

Dave slapped the top of his car. He'd run shine while he was in high school, been trained in an academy that thought they knew everything, and this was the first time he'd heard of this one.

"I hope they paid you enough to make it worthwhile." He grinned at Granny. "I'm tempted to arrest you right now!"

CHAPTER 5

"You're going to pay!" Granny yelled.

"Aw come on! Knock it off! We both know your job is over and done!"

Granny stopped with the finger up in the air.

Dave couldn't help but grin. "Relax, you did a good job. There is no way I can catch that car now." The grin disappeared. "Of course when I do catch them and get them to admit they paid you to purposely block the road I'll be coming for you. How long would two years in prison be to you?"

Granny dropped the finger and climbed into the old truck. It cranked the instant she touched the starter. She backed it up the driveway. Climbing stiffly from the cab she walked back into the light. She bent over and held the finger up and stuck her tongue out. "So long mister Revenoor, I'll see you next trip."

Dave drove slowly away. There was no reason to hurry. He knew he'd never catch the Ford now. At least he now knew what kind of car to look for. When he'd come through the dust on the inside of the turn he'd had the barest glimpse of the human form behind the wheel. Something about it gnawed at the back of his mind. He hadn't even got a good glance but something about it gnawed on him.

Lizzy hurled through the night. She was shaken to her toes. She never dreamed the Internal Revenue Service possessed a car or driver equal to the one who pursued her tonight. If it hadn't been for Granny Whooten ... She shuddered. She would deliver this load and leave the car sit for a few days. She'd borrow another car for the return trip.

She didn't like to leave the Ford but knew the Feds would be looking for it on the way back. It seemed a desecration to park the loaner Pontiac in the small barn across from the school.

It was a slim trim Miss Lesa Turner who sat behind the desk and said hello to the class the next morning. The hair was back in the bun on the back of her neck. There was no indication of the Lizzy Turner of the night before.

Pots stirred the mash. It was a perfect day to make moonshine. The temperature was right. The conditions soured the mash quickly and a gentle breeze scattered the thin trial of smoke that rose from the fire box.

"What are we going to do now that Lizzy is taking a few days off?" Joe Jay stuck the bung in an oak barrel. We'll have a load tonight. I'm going to be happy when this run is done. Those Feds are too getting to active to suit me."

"Aw, we'll get Louis or Billy Jack to run it. I think Lizzy got the big eyes on that car chasing her. It will be better to have several cars run out of here anyway. It will sort of spread things out. Make it harder for the Feds."

"I'm sure glad it's somebody beside me driving that fast on those dark roads." Joe Joe chimed in.

Three days later Lesa sat in her usual place to greet the students. Jeff hurried up to her desk. "Miss Turner." He said breathlessly. "The Feds got Louis last night. He's in jail. They got him with a full load." He rushed on. "The Judge set his bail so high he can't get out of jail."

Charlie's cabin was buried deep in the mountains south of the valley. Charlie was a solitary man. He lived alone except for a small ragamuffin dog. At five foot ten the strength of the huge shoulders and hands belied his sixty years. One of the things that kept him fit was the exercise he got carrying the five guns he always wore. There was one in each boot, two on the belt and a tiny one behind his belt buckle. Always wild, the brown eyes would turn absolutely feral when he was riled. The man behind the eyes was as feral as the eyes. There was a saying among the valley folks, "If you have trouble with Charlie shoot first and argue later."

The still produced a little more whiskey than Charlie could drink. The small amount of money from the still gave him a meager existence. It bought bullets for his guns, chewing tobacco; etc most of the food he ate came from the river bottoms or the mountains. He had no electric or gas bill and after one trip into mountains the tax collectors were more than happy to forget him. About the only people he ever saw were the locals who were his customers. His trips into town were limited to once or twice a year. This fact the Sheriff was very thankful for. The Sheriff and both his Deputies had to be on full twenty hour alert when Charlie was in town.

Compete solitude honed Charlie's senses. He could feel a human approaching his cabin long before they got within sight of it.. A contest developed among the local people to see if anyone could sneak up on Charlie at home. Men and boys vied for the honor of catching Charlie unawares at his cabin. Very accomplished woodsmen tried. All failed. Charlie was always laying in ambush for anyone who tried to creep up on him. He always ambushed the ambushers. Dave felt there was a tragedy in the making here. If Charlie made a mistake and decided one of the pranksters was a Revenue Agent there would be blood on the rocks.

The cabin sat high on a long rocky point which ran down into the river bottom. Large Yellow Pines and Post Oaks spilled down the point to clash with the huge Red Oaks rooted into the rich bottomland. It was a windy location but it furnished a great view. No one could approach the cabin unseen. A clear rock walled spring on the hill above the cabin sang a song with the water falling over the wall. Clear cold water boiled out of the spring in abundance. Far more water than Charlie or his still could ever use.

Charlie sat on a block of wood and listened to the symphony of the forest. It was sweeter music than man was capable of producing. This tune was Charlie's solace and protection. Everything that moves poses some sort of threat to another Denison of the forest. When threatened, the specimen would alter or stop his love song. Charlie's ears were attuned to every nuance of this tune. If a note altered or stopped his ear picked up the change and his mind examined it. He grew so keen on who's song stopped or who whistled a warning for a given thing that he not only knew something was coming before it came into his sight, he knew what was coming. He could tell whether it was dog, fox, coyote, deer or man. Man was the easiest to detect. All the forest folks feared and distrusted man.

There was no electricity, no TV, no radio, no humming motors or electronic interference. The air he breathed was pure and clear mountain air. The freedom from pollution allowed Charlie's sense of smell to develop. He could smell a human half mile upwind of him.

Even when he was asleep Charlie's ears stayed tuned. If the rhythm of the forest altered or stopped it set off an alarm bell in his mind. When the alarm woke Charlie he was fully awake, instantly. He needed no yawning or stretching time to wake up. Nothing would change when he woke up. Even the heavy breathing continued while his nose and ears checked out the reason for the alarm. An observer could never tell the instant he awoke. If it was a threat he was ready to react immediately. If it was something frivolous he went back to sleep instantly.

He was leaning back against a log. His ears were flowing with the symphony of the forest and enjoying the solitude when the corner of his eye caught the rising dust. He turned and watched the dust boil up beyond the second mountain to the south. An automobile was coming. Considering the rough condition of the road and the distance it would be at least a half an hour before they arrived.

Charlie looked around and decided he was as ready for company as he was going get, be it customer or the Feds. No one else would come this far into Charlie's domain.

Charlie grinned when the beat up old Chevrolet topped the last rise. It was a bunch of the local boys. They were a boisterous, noisy and rowdy group but they were among the few people Charlie liked to see coming. Their exuberance touched some forgotten cord of the past. He knew they pooled their money, scraped and scratched to get enough together to buy a pint. By the time the pint was passed around there was about enough for a long shot apiece. They felt they were being grown up and very bad at the same time. Charlie limited their purchase to a pint. It always seemed that was all the whiskey he could spare when they were around.

The old car stopped and boys boiled out of it. Some came through the doors and some through the windows.

"What are you sorry boys up to today?" Charlie smiled for the first time in weeks.

"Well, things were getting pretty dry so we came over to see if you had anything to drink." Leroy was a tall lanky boy just coming out of the awkward stage.

Charlie looked across the tops of the pine covered ridges and made up his mind. Holding a palm out he crossed it with a forefinger. "It has to rain before the creek can run", he said.

Leroy laid the price for a pint in his hand. They wanted more but knew a pint was all he'd sell them.

Charlie turned to the cabin. "You boys come in here I want to show you something."

The cabin was a fair sized one room affair. One corner served as a kitchen. Another corner was the bedroom. There were chairs of mixed size, shape and vintages scattered around the room. Charlie walked to the far wall to make room for the boys to get into the room.

"I'm going to sell you boys a pint but you all be real careful. The Revenoors are sneaking around here."

"What makes you say that?" Leroy was skeptical.

"The Feds were up here last night. One peeped in that window over there." Charlie made an off hand wave toward the window.

Jake walked to the window. "Boy, somebody sure blew this window out." He ran his eyes around the window frame and looked at the glass scattered across the yard.

"I did. A Revenoor tried to peep through it. I could have killed him but I decided to teach him a lesson." Charlie laughed; he remembered the expression on the Revenoor's face when he saw the twin holes of a double barrel twelve gauge six inches from his nose. "I held a little high and you ought to have seen him when she roared and the glass went crashing into his face. Them big double ought buckshot stir up a pretty good fuss on a still night."

"Are you sure it was a Revenoor?" Leroy was having trouble believing a Revenue Agent would turn into a peeping tom.

Charlie turned to the dresser. Picking up something he turned to the boys again. "Did you ever see anybody in this valley smoke a cigar this expensive?" He triumphantly waved four long cigars. "He fell and lost these cigars. Then he fell again and lost these." Charlie picked up an expensive pair of gold frame glasses and held them in front of his eyes. "Come to think of, it that boy was having trouble keeping on his feet. He fell about every time that shotgun popped."

Charlie slipped the glasses onto his face and looked around. Raising his hands he examined them carefully. "Hey!" He exclaimed. "Them Feds did me a favor sneaking in here. I got me four cigars, a pocket knife, a hair comb, a handful of change, set of keys and a pair of good eye glasses out of the deal. What do you think boys? Should I invite them back?" He removed the glasses, elevated and admired them. "I wonder what he'll think when he sees me wearing these."

Two weeks before Charlie's episode the director called all the agents to a conference at his office. It was a large lavishly furnished corner office. A huge mahogany desk reflected the original oil paintings on three walls and the awards, plagues, commendations and other trinkets bestowed on the Director by his superior officers and a grateful public for the hard work his field agents did. A harsh light came through the big windows behind and beside the director to bounce off the shiny desktop.

The director occupied a big black overstuffed armed office chair behind the desk. The agents sat in a semi-circle around the desk in the most uncomfortable chairs the director could find. The director ordered everyone who came into the office to sit. It was below his dignity to look up at any man while conversing with him and the Director was not going to stand when he had such an imposing desk to sit behind. It was his throne. For the rest of the office he selected chairs so uncomfortable no one would want to sit in them any longer than absolutely necessary.

"I want a report from each of you. Why haven't you shut the stills down and arrested someone." The director shifted the small spectacles and pinched the nose he always stared down.

"The governor's office told me bootleggers burned an informant's barns and poisoned his cattle. The informant was forced to move out of the valley in order to keep his family safe."

"We've arrested a major whiskey runner and intercepted a load of whiskey crossing the state line." Chester shifted in his chair. "This is a major blow to the bootleggers. They're going to have to make up for the load we have taken from them."

"We've located the still and raided the pile of ashes where it sat several times. They have been making whiskey on the fly. They've managed to move the still before we can raid it." Harold picked thoughtfully at his finger nail. "Perhaps we need to change our raiding techniques. We're getting there too slow."

"We have to follow proper procedure so what we find will stand up in court." The director was a hide bound book man. He couldn't go with the flow and change with the situation. "We've got to arrest someone. A fish I can throw to my superiors."

Dave raised his head. "The more we mess with the small fry the longer it will take us to get the big boys. We can catch the big boys and shut down the small fry later. If we catch the big boys most of the small fry will shut down. It could save a lot of friction with the mountain people."

"Nevertheless let's arrest someone. I have information there is an old hermit living in the mountains and peddling booze to young boys." The director turned to Dave. "One of the boys is sweet on a town girl. He bragged to her he could buy whiskey anytime he wanted. Her dad is less than thrilled with the boy as a suitor so he is putting pressure on me to arrest both the man and the boy."

"That would be Charlie Winters." Dave said thoughtfully. "He mostly makes what he can drink. The small excess he sells to the locals. He doesn't sell any booze across the river."

"You know someone is bootlegging and you haven't arrested them?" The Director turned on Dave.

"The only evidence we have is this girl's dad claiming the boy told her." Dave didn't like the proposition.

"I want you to look through his window and if you can see any whiskey we'll arrest him. It shouldn't be too hard and we can show we're doing something."

"My orders were to stop the flow of whiskey across the river. We are on the verge of doing that. Don't pull us off and let us lose time with a small fry like Charlie. Besides it's not going to be as simple as you think it will be. Old Charlie may be a hermit but he is a respected member of the community and he is a rough tough old buzzard. He won't surrender. He will go down fighting.

"Anyone crawling up to his shack in order to look through the window is going to get a bait of buckshot for supper and it isn't going to be me!" Dave had his dander up.

"Are you refusing to arrest a bootlegger?" The Director's head went back and he looked down the double barreled nose again.

"No, I'm not! You give me a warrant and I'll arrest Charlie and you give me a search warrant I'll tear his place apart." Dave paused for breath. "What I'm refusing to do is perform an illegal act and get myself killed in the process. You're a book man. Stop and think about this. This can't be done at Charlie's house. Let me get him at Harper's store. He's sure to have a jug with him when he comes in.

"Any man in the valley will shoot a peeking tom and rightly so."

The director kept sucking air and sputtering. His face turned redder and redder. He was building up to the explosion point. Dave's face set and his eyes glittered. He intended to give no ground on this point.

"I'll do it," Harold, the bespectacled mildest of the group stepped into the gap.

"Ok, the rest of you will back him up." The director deflated.

Dave gave it one more try. "The only way he stands a chance is to go alone. If he decides to arrest Charlie we can back him up. We'll need all the backup we can get. This is not going to be as easy as you think."

"Are you refusing to backup a fellow officer?" The Director began to swell again

"No Sir! I'm trying to use some common sense." Dave was ready to toss his badge on the desk and walk out.

It was a clear moonless night with a steady little breeze blowing. It was a perfect night for the mission. The stars gave enough light to move around by and without the moon there were no harsh shadows to give anyone's presence away. The breeze would carry their scent downwind. Could Charlie smell them? These after shave lotion, deodorant wearing, cigar smoking men would trip Charlie's sense of smell a half mile downwind. Charlie had always lived where the air was clear, clean and pine scented.

CHAPTER 6

Dave insisted they park the vehicles five miles from Charlie's shack and walk in. They stopped behind the last ridge.

"No talking beyond this point." Dave said softly. "Not even a whisper." He turned to Harold. "If he looks like he's reading or concentrating on something back out immediately. He's located you."

It took the group an hour to creep the last quarter mile to the clearing. A kerosene lamp cast a soft glow through the window. This was good. Harold would be able to see the inside of the cabin and the light would impede Charlie's vision into the darkness. Charlie had hauled a load of wood and dumped it on the downwind side of the clearing about halfway between the house and the trees. This was good. It would give Harold some cover halfway to the window and give him a place to dive behind if things got hot.

Dave's hand made a straight line motion to the woodpile then a circular around the pile motion and another straight line to the wall beside the window. If it hadn't been for Dave's convictions Harold would have been feeling good about the mission. He'd spent four years in a Marine Corp Special Forces Group. Infiltration was a specialty with him. In view of Dave's worries he paid close attention to his camouflage and moved across the clearing with infinite care.

Harold reached the wall and eased up to peek through the lower corner of the window. He saw a blur of movement inside. Then his eyes focused on the huge black holes in the business end of a twelve gauge double barreled shotgun! He tried to duck. The glass exploded in his face. A thunderclap, the magnitude of which he'd never heard before assaulted his ears. The concussion knocked him down. The pressure on his ears was unbearable.

He lucked out and blinked a movement before the blast. His eyes were closed when the shattered glass hit him. He had cuts where the glass hit his face but the closed eyelids kept the flying glass shards out of his eyes.

Dazed, Harold panicked. Leaping to his feet he ran a few steps, tripped and fell. The muzzle blast from the shotgun assaulted his ears again. It wasn't as bad now as it had been when it was almost in his face. In his panic Harold ran into the woodpile.

When Harold hit the woodpile he went down again. All the stuff flew out of his pockets. Every time he leaped up a stick of the wood rolled under him or grabbed his foot and he would go down again. He fell with every blast of the shotgun. The buckshot whistled, chucked, and thwacked the trees and brush all around Dave and Chester.

At the first blast Chester raised his rifle to shoot at the window. Dave slapped the barrel down. "Don't shoot!" He bellowed. "He's playing with Harold now if he'd wanted him dead he would have killed him first shot. If you shoot now and miss Charlie, Harold won't stand a chance! Charlie's next shot won't be for fun."

Harold reached them. He was in a daze. His ears were ringing from the concussions and he was in shock. The damage to his ears threw his balance off.

"I'm going in after the son-of-____!" Chester began.

"No you ain't." Dave grabbed Chester's arm.

"Yes I am!" Chester jerked his arm.

"He isn't in there anymore!" Dave grabbed Chester's gun.

"Where is he?" Chester began to understand.

"He's out here in the dark with us. It's up to him now whether any of us make it back to the car alive." Dave took Harold by the hand and began leading him toward the car. Dave's flesh crawled. Goose bumps marched to and fro on his skin. A spot between his shoulder blades tingled. He could feel the cold hand of retribution coming out of the shadowy darkness.

Would it be a flash of fire in the dark? The thump of big buckshot driving home, ripping flesh, breaking bone, destroying organs and it all would be over? Or would Charlie opt to use the blade so he could inflict more pain? The razor sharp, silent, deadly blade, would it come with a sharp pain in the bowels with the blade ripping upward into the chest? Would it come as a sharp pain between the shoulders when the blade drove into vital organs? How about a sharp sting across the neck so you could stand and dumbly watch your life's blood spurt out? The once friendly shifting shadows now became mortal enemies. Each shadow could harbor instant death. Or would it be instant? Perhaps they would be left to slowly bleed out in the soft darkness. It depends on how mad Charlie is he decided.

If Charlie killed all three of them no one would ever know for sure who did the killing. If it was found that Charlie did the killing he'd say they were prowlers and they were carrying guns. Dave knew Charlie was both mentally and physically capable of killing all three of them. Dave's hand instinctively tightened on the service .45 in his hand. He walked with the safety off. There would be no time to get it into action but who knows; even a rat will fight a cat as long as he lives.

The silent stars were brilliant in the night sky. A gentle breeze nudged the tree tops into motion. A fox barked down the creek. Dave flinched at the sound. An owl hooted upstream. Was it an owl or was it human? All the hillbillies used owl language to communicate with each other. They were so good you had to know the sound of a person's voice to differentiate between the hillbilly and a real owl. Dave stopped to listen. The owl hooted again. Dave could find nothing distinguishable about it. Did Charlie have someone with him tonight? It was unlikely but if Charlie had company it made their chances of getting out alive even slimmer. Dave's imagination began seeing fleeting figures between shadows. Or was it his imagination?

The crescendo of the cicadas, the chirp of the crickets, and the call of the whippoorwill overrode by the yelp of a coyote. The night woods are never silent. Silence is a void and Mother Nature will not tolerate a void.

Dave's ears grappled with the natural sounds. They were trying to sort the sounds of the night and pick up a sound he knew he'd never hear, a sound he surely did not want to hear, the sound of Charlie moving in the dark.

A doe leaped away down the ridge. Dave froze at the sound, his heart pounding. He expected a flash of light and the terrible blow of a load of buckshot piercing the skin. After a few heart pounding seconds Dave started Harold moving again.

Dave had no illusions as to whether Charlie would kill them or not. Charlie didn't care if they were Federal Agents. If he thought it was to his advantage or if he got mad enough he'd have no qualms about killing them. "Just like three weasels in my hen house." Charlie would say. No one would find the bodies. They would not be the first person Charlie ground up and fed to the pigs. Dave shuttered. The thought of being eaten by pigs was worse than the thought of getting killed.

They stumbled on through the ominous shadowy forest. The shotgun blast severely damaged Harold's ears. His balance was off. He couldn't walk on the dark, rough trail by himself. Dave supported him on one side and Chester the other. Due to this they were forced to travel very slowly. Harold was somewhat recovered by the time they arrived at the automobiles.

The hoods were up. Someone had reached in with a big knife and cut wiring indiscriminately. The windshield and side glasses were broken and all the tires were slashed. The headlights were broken out. The seat covers were cut to shreds. A pair of Charlie's dirty drawers hung on one of the mirrors. Dave smiled in relief. It was over. Charlie had his final say on the matter. They were safe now.

"Thank god he took it out on the cars." Dave leaned on a car to rest a minute before walking on. "If Charlie had come after us we would look like these cars."

"What do you mean, he got away?" The Director

screamed. "Can't three Internal Revenue Service Agents handle one old has been?"

"Not from the position you put us in." Dave was mad.

"I'll turn out the agency! I'll get the boys from the academy! We'll go get that old goat!" The Director was pacing a circle. A twitch began at the corner of his mouth.

"No you won't. If you send a bunch of those boys into the mountains you will get a lot of good men killed and you might not get Charlie even then." Dave smiled a grim smile. "What are you going after him for anyway? Firing a few shots around a peeping tom?" Dave smiled again at the Director's agitation. "I don't think that will impress a jury. The damage to the cars was vandalism. He has a clean record so even if you could prove he did it probation is the worst you could do to him.

"If you start a big manhunt all the news media will pick it up and we'll all look like the idiots we are. If I was you I'd have Harold treated for the damage he suffered in the accident and write the cars off."

Dave sat for a minute. "I'll catch Charlie with something that counts later. You don't go after people like Charlie on their own grounds."

While the Feds were occupied with Charlie, Lizzy made two uneventful runs across the river. While the whiskey tanks were being drained and bottled, Lizzy sat at a table in the corner of the garage conversing with Ted Pilcher, the middleman. She was growing more and more irritated by his leering arrogant air.

"You go back and tell them boys I'll send their money up with the next load." The deal was winding down and Ted was playing with ideas.

"You do that and the next load you get will be a chunk of lead delivered by a 30-30 rifle." Lizzy took a sip of her pop.

"I was thinking I'd keep you and the money this trip." He leaned an elbow on the table and leered at her.

"I know you don't want to do that." Lizzy laughed. "Why?"

Lizzy leaned over the table and looked him in

the eyes. "Because I'd gut shoot you and I'd castrate you before you died." She growled. "I don't know where you think you are going with this but take some advice and deal straight up. You haven't even dreamed of the hell you will be in if you double cross them boys up yonder. If they didn't kill what was left of you I would." The unblinking cold gray eyes glittered with frost.

Ted's stomach leaped up and grabbed him by the throat. He made involuntary movements with his hands. He had never been so deeply shocked in his life. Those cold frosty gray eyes glittered with a feral gleam and continued to burn into his brain. He was like a rat caught in the baleful glare of a rattler. His mind was begging for release but his feet couldn't move. If the women were this tough, how tough would the men be? Ted chucked all the plans and air castles he'd been toying with.

"I don't like the idea!" Pots made a chopping motion and turned around.

"I'm going to take some time off from this. I think we should wait until the heats off." Lizzy was quiet but firm. "Ted Pilcher is up to something. I don't know what but he has something in mind. He was feeling me out."

"What do you think he's up to?" Pots demanded.

"I don't know but he was thinking of not paying you boys for the last load. I convinced him it wouldn't be a good idea to jip you. We're close to fulfilling the amount of whiskey we said we'd deliver. Even if they didn't buy the rest later it would be better than having Dave Miloy snapping handcuffs on us."

"We've made enough money to live on for awhile. It might be best to shut the still down for the time being. We nearly got caught last time we moved the still. Miloy keeps getting closer and closer." Joe Joe spoke for the first time.

"At first I thought if we stopped Miloy would move on to some other place." Joe Jay leaned against a tree. "But I think he's going to stay now. He bought the Banner's place yesterday."

"You have got to be kidding me! Doesn't he know that place can burn?" Pots face turned red.

"He couldn't be that dumb."

"I'd think that over real carefully. It's one thing to burn and run a city feller out of the valley and another to try burning Dave Miloy out." Joe Jay had apparently spent some time thinking about it. "In the first place Dave is a Federal Agent. Burning his place would be a federal crime. Now the Sheriff won't come up here but the Feds will.

"Me and Joe Joe went to school with Dave. I've fought him a time or two. I think he will come back to his raising. I don't think he will run. If we start this with him I think there will be blood and ashes on our places. Him being a Federal Agent I think he's got the edge on us with the law." Joe Jay looked Pots in the eye. "I don't think we should do this now but if we do anything we should kill him."

Lizzy's head snapped around. "Kill him? You have to be joking! That would bring the Feds down in force."

"It could be done." Pots rubbed his jaw, "if it was done right."

"We'd have to lay low for a long time." Joe Jay

added.

"I don't believe this! I cannot believe we are having this conversation. Count me out of this deal. I won't have any part of it!" Lizzy was adamant

"You are already part of it. You've been running back and forth across the river." Pots said.

"What I've been doing isn't taking somebody's life. The worst they will do if I get caught crossing the river is two to four years in a federal prison. Most likely it wouldn't be that much. Most likely be probation." Lizzy rose from the rock. "What you're talking about is the Electric Chair. And they will hunt for you a lot harder than they have hunted me. Count me out!" Lizzy walked off.

There was a long silence while the men ran the situation through their minds.

"Liz is a different girl but sometimes she makes sense. Count me out." Joe Joe followed Liz. After a few steps he turned. "Joe Jay, you better think this one out carefully."

CHAPTER 7

D ave eased the black car off the road and let it grumble its way to the door. The extra wide tires crunched the gravel. When it came to a stop Dave revved the engine to burn the overload it picked up coming in. There was a sudden roar and then the popping back rap of a big engine. The whine of the super charger stopped when he turned the key off.

Stepping out and admiring the car Dave smiled. He let the screen door bang shut behind him when he entered Harper's store. He walked back to the spit and whittle chairs around the cold stove. He took a seat facing the door. He wanted to sit and think. He wanted people to see him and do some thinking on their own. The old days were over. The world was changing and like it or not this valley was going to change with it. The days of making whiskey as an occupation were severely numbered.

Harper lay on the counter on a sack of gray shorts hog feed. He'd lain on this same sack for twenty-five years. It was beat down to fit his exact contour. Turning to dangle his feet over the counter he sat up and looked at Dave. Neither man spoke. After a few moments passed Harper slid off the counter and strolled to the cold drink box. Pulling a Dr. Pepper from the cold water of the case he popped the lid and strolled past Dave. He handed the Dr. Pepper to Dave and returned to his sack on the counter.

Dave sat and meditated for some time. The Dr. Pepper had been almost consumed.

"You remembered." Dave waved the Dr. Pepper at Harper.

"Yeah."

"Aren't you afraid some of your upright customers will see me drink it in the store?" Dave was sarcastic.

"I've had this store for over twenty-five years and I've never took sides in a local feud. I always stay clear of them. I hear you bought Jim Banner's place. That makes you a local again. I wondered what was going to happen to the place when Jim and Matilda moved to California. None of their kids will ever live in this valley again. They got a taste of the big money. Welcome home and I sure hope you didn't forget the things you learned while you were growing up." Harper talked himself out of breath.

A red Chevrolet pickup wheeled onto the parking spaces in front of the store. Dave got a momentary glance at Vera Lee. It was like a prayer answered. He hoped he'd get a chance to talk to her, to explain his side and his feelings. Was this the real reason he was at Harper's store? He rose and took two involuntary steps forward.

The screen door opened and Vera Lee stepped through it and stopped instantly. She is prettier than ever, Dave thought. "Vera." Dave began taking two more steps forward. Vera stepped back and slammed the screen door. "Lee," Dave finished lamely.

Dave's jaw was hanging. He turned back to Mr. Harper.

"Don't look at me. I'm only seventy. I've not been on this earth long enough to figure women out." Harper shrugged both shoulders.

The screen door spring sang again and Lesa entered carrying a basket on her arm. She handed the basket and a list to Harper. Harper busied himself putting stuff into the basket.

"Is that your car out there?" Lesa queried.

"Yep." Dave pushed a chair toward her.

She hesitated and sat down. "It looks fast."

"Do you know a lot about fast cars?" Dave watched her eyes.

"My dad was a driver on the race circuits until he was killed in a flaming accident. I learned what a fast car looks like. I don't know anything about the workings of one." Her eyes told Dave a different story.

"This one has 60 thousandth over sized eleven to

one pistons. The crank stroke has been cut down till the engine is a little under square. It has a Mallory dual point distributor, dual Coldfield high voltage coils, high lift long duration cam, and a Ray Jay Super Charger." Dave watched her carefully. He knew she understood what each part was. She didn't ask questions about any of it.

"That certainly sounds like a lot of parts. Will it run?" She asked demurely.

"Your order is ready Miss Turner." Harper heaved the full basket up on the counter.

"Do you want to find out?" Dave picked up the basket.

"Well," this was the car she was going to be competing with perhaps she could find a weakness she could exploit in the future. "For a short while."

The car blasted out onto the county road with singing pipes. Dave threw it into the first curve in a great cloud of dust. Recovering from the turn Dave threw the car into a bootlegger turn. 180 degrees at speed and slide backward with the wheels spinning forward until the momentum bled off and the car started moving forward again.

Lesa sat relaxed with a smile on her face. The wild maneuvers never fazed her. "Reminds me of my father," she said without guile. "Drop me at the store." She'd found out what she wanted to know. She had a formidable opponent in both car and driver. "There's a pie supper at the school next Saturday. Why don't you come?" Lesa could have kicked herself. What did she do that for?

Dave mulled it over. "I might do that. I want the people of this country to see me. I want them to realize I 'm here and I intend to stay. We're going to clean this valley up. The still, as a means of living, is a thing of the past." He looked her in the eyes. "They can win many times. We only have to win once and someone gets a long vacation."

In the following weeks Dave, Harold and Chester busted several small stills. Dave knew the big still had gone to ground. He also knew it would start up again. All they had to do was wait and hope for a break.

One raid only consisted of Chester and Dave. It

was a hardscrabble old place consisting of a board and bat heart of pine house and a rickety old barn with a spilt board roof. Inside this barn was a makeshift still and one gallon of illegal whiskey. The worm was constructed from an old car radiator.

They arrested the tall gaunt hillbilly who was past middle age and chained him to the snubbing post in the barnyard. Terry Midler was thin almost to the point of emaciation. His Galloused overalls flopped on him like loose sails on a ship. His long hair fell in his face and the handcuffs on his wrists prevented moving it back.

Chester approached the still with an axe. He paused to look at it once more. "Would you drink whiskey made on this contraption? I especially enjoy chopping up one of these." Chester fell to with a will. Dave helped and they chopped until they were sure the still was beyond repair.

`When they emerged from the barn a lady in a long loose shift was standing with Terry. "Will you let Terry eat before he leaves?"

"We don't have time." Chester was fishing the

keys from his pocket.

"It won't take long I already have it cooked. You fellows come and eat too."

Chester was going to refuse again.

"Please mister. Terry ain't et since yesterday. You can eat with him then there won't be any wasted time."

Chester looked at Dave. Dave smiled. "It might do you some good to eat a hillbilly meal if you want. I'm keeping this jug between my feet. We sure don't want to lose our evidence do we?"

The table was long and there was a bench on both sides of it. Scattered down these benches were ten children of stair stepped ages. They were all silent and staring at these Demons in their midst.

Terry sat at the head of the table. Chester and Dave sat on the end of the bench on each side of the table. They were within arms reach of Terry on either side.

Dave surveyed the table. There was a bowl of fried squirrel, a bowl of Polk salad, a bowl of sour dock and lamb's quarter greens cooked together.

There were ten silent white faces that weren't eating although they looked like they needed it. Twenty scared, sad eyes never left his face. Each eye mirrored fear of the dreaded Revenoors. These eyes were watching him eat the last of their food. While he sat there the line of white faces seemed to grow longer and the number of eyes seamed to increase. He could feel the eyes drilling into him. Each time he looked up they were there, unblinking.

Why did he ever become an Internal Revenue Agent anyway? Dave thought back to his childhood days. If the Revenoors had come after his dad he would have been as petrified as these children were. Every Revenoor was a devil with four horns. Not one child touched a morsel of food.

Dave eyed the oldest boy. Was he old enough to take over the chores and wild game food gathering chores his father performed up to this point? He doubted the youngster was up to it. These children grew quick because it was necessary. They took a hand in the chores and work at a tender age. Dave himself had been driving a team of mules hooked to a go-devil plowing corn before he was old enough to see the inside of a school house.

The mousy little woman looked like she had been burned out by the fires of child birth, hard work and too little food.

Dave sampled the polk salad and sour dock just for old time's sake. He left the squirrel alone because even though the children had not taken a piece there wasn't enough to go around.

"You know she cooked the best and all she had." Dave looked down the table at the sad eyes again. They were afraid. And they hated him for what he was in the process of doing.

Chester nodded.

"You know all this came from the woods don't you?" Dave asked Chester.

"Yeah, and these greens aren't half bad. I'm going to pay her for the meal."

"No you won't pay her for the meal. She won't accept it." Dave was positive.

"I'll lose twenty dollars on the way to the truck."

"It won't work."

"Why? It's obvious they need it."

"Pride, they don't have much else but they will guard that pride to the death."

Chester leaned an elbow on the table and looked down the row of white faces with the accusing eyes. "You do what you want. I'm with you all the way." Turning his back to Dave he rose and walked away from the table.

Dave's feet moved. There was a thunk and a gurgling sound. Dave rose and looked at the wet floor. "I'll be damned!" Dave exclaimed. "Chester, I've spilled all our evidence."

When he removed the chains from Terry's legs Dave rose and lay a friendly hand on Terry's shoulder. "If I have to come up here again I'll ask the Judge for twenty years."

"I'll do better than that I'll ask him for forty years." Chester sounded like he meant it.

Later, the headlights burned a hole in the velvety blackness of the night. Darkness was a time to rest. It hid the pride of things accomplished today, the nagging sight of things to be accomplished tomorrow and the ugliness of things that would never be accomplished.

Dave swung around a baby rabbit and the lights settled on a fawn standing in the middle of the road. The lights reflected brightly off the white spots scattered randomly across its body. Dave kicked the clutch in and revved the big engine. The resulting roar and popping back rap and the flashes of flame from the exhaust pipes panicked the fawn. He went looking for mama. He was so alarmed he was jumping three feet high but only covered two feet forward. Dave sat chuckling. The fawn bobbed up and down like a ping pong ball. The little fellow finally cleared the ditch and disappeared into the darkness.

Dave idled down the road looking for more wildlife. Centuries ago most prey animals realized the most voracious predator of all, man, was not developing eyes with good night vision and became nocturnal themselves. All the predators except man and most of the bird world developed night vision and followed the prey animals.

Rolling along through the darkness Dave wondered if Vera Lee would be there. Sure she would be there; the pie supper was one of the big social events of the valley. There was no way the queen bee could miss it. What if she was with another man? Dave steeled himself against this event. What difference did it make anyway? She made it very clear she had no interest in him.

Dave's heart failed him and he was about to turn back when the lights of the school hovered into sight. No, he told himself savagely, I'm going to convince these people I'm here to stay and I'm going to do my job.

The pie supper was in full swing when Dave parked the black car. The old school brought back many memories, both good and bad. He'd attended school here the first eight years. Mrs. Hightower laid a sound foundation for him to build on for the next ten years. She instilled the industry and joy of learning that propelled him to the top of his class in High School, College and the Academy.

He walked a circle of the parking lot. He noticed

several of the vehicles had a jar lying in the seat. This didn't bother him too much. If all the stills were dried up there would be more bonded whiskey lying around. At least the tax would be paid on it.

Vera Lee stood near the door. She looked shocked at his entrance then very deliberately raised her nose and turned her back. Primping her hair she engaged in conversation with the man in front of her. Others followed her example. Most either didn't see him or were not interested in the fact he was in the building. Lesa was engaged in conversation across the room but she was watching for him. She floated across the floor and staked a claim on his arm. "You're just in time. The pie sale is about to begin. My box is the one with a big red bow on top and little red bows on the side." She led him across the room to the group she was standing with when he came in. Some people gave him a curt nod. Others moved away.

Vera Lee took in a sharp breath, almost a gasp, when she realized Lesa's mission across the room was going to end at Dave. This wouldn't do. Dave belonged to her. Vera Lee had plans for Dave. She would ignore him until he begged. After he begged a proper amount of time she'd grant him a little time to get him hooked solidly then she would spring the ultimatum, either me or the Internal Revenue Service. She was sure she would prevail. She'd been worried by the long absence while he was away at the Academy. When he came to her house looking for her she knew she had him.

Her father running him off and telling her to never speak to him didn't matter.

In fact it played into her hand. When she decided to take Dave back into her good graces she could explain her reaction to him. She had ignored him because she was obeying her father.

Now this teacher was interfering. This, this Jezebel latched onto Dave like she owned an interest. Well we will see about this! It took all her will power not to follow Lesa and Dave across the room.

"Ladies and Gentlemen," Harper held a microphone at the teacher's desk. "It has been decided the proceeds from this pie supper is going to buy land and improve the cemetery. If there are any funds left over they will be turned over to the School Board. Now you buckaroos count the pennies in your pocket and ask the girl what her box looks like." Harper paused while the laughter died down. No one was supposed to know what box belonged to which lady until it was sold.

Vera's mother sat a box on the front edge of the teacher's desk.

"Now let's begin the sale." Harper wandered toward the box on the desk. "We have a pretty little box here." Harper stopped and waved his nose in the air like a hound dog hunting a trial then bent over the box. He rose and threw both hands up. "Boys you ought to smell this box. One smell and you'd turn your pocket's wrong side out. That is southern fried chicken or my name is Doug Hiemershild." There was a round of laughter. It was the same every pie supper. Entertainment was scarce in the hills and this was for a good cause.

"Ok what do I have bid on this box?" Harper held it high so everyone could see.

"Fifty cents." This came from a large country boy leaning on a window facing.

Mr. Harper's face took on a shocked look and he turned to face the wall behind him. When he turned back he had a supplicating condescending look and held out one hand. "Now Dick," he asked. "Would you insult the pretty little lady who spent so much time and effort to bring this meal to perfection, with a bid that low?"

The crowd laughed and Dick turned red. "Seventy five cants." He corrected.

Mr. Harper stood full height and pulled the microphone in close. "Well now, that is somewhat better. I have seventy five who will give me a dollar?"

"One dollar," floated up from the crowd. And the auction droned on with Harper adding comic relief from time to time.

"Now folks, I want you to look at this box! Have you ever seen anything prettier? One big red bow on top and small red bows on all sides, those bows alone ought to be worth five dollars." Harper looked at the crowd.

"Five dollars." Dave bid. Every one chuckled because this was the highest bid of the night. Vera Lee huffed up and turned purple. She expected Dave to buy her box. Of course she was planning to refuse to eat it with him. He'd let her box sell without placing a single bid on it. Her box sold for the handsome sum of one dollar and she was forced to eat it with the country bumpkin who lived next door. There was one consolation. He had a crush on her and she could lead him around by the nose.

"Ten dollars," everyone turned to see Pots standing straddle legged by the door, head tipped forward, fist balled and resting on his hips.

Mr. Harper hesitated. He didn't like the looks of this but he could see no way out. "Ten, I have ten dollar, how about eleven?

"Fifteen dollars." Dave held up a hand.

"He is drunk and dangerous." Lesa whispered so softly only Dave could hear.

"Twenty dollars!" Pots roared stepping forward.

Harper held his peace and stared at the men. He hoped Dave had taken his advice about remembering his mountain raising seriously. Pots was fifty pound heavier than Dave. He figured that if he got Dave into a fight over a girl and killed him the country folk could understand this. The Sheriff would do nothing. The Feds? Well he'd have to take his chances there. This would be a job related fight.

All talk ceased in the crowd. People shifted until they could see both men. This left a lane open between them.

"One hundred dollars!" Dave held one finger up to Harper and starred at Pots.

Pots only had fifty dollars. It didn't make any difference. He planned to kill Dave in the fight anyway. The fight would have taken place if the final bid had been one dollar.

"Why you badge toting SOB." Pots made as if to turn away and launched a hay maker at Dave. Dave waited nonchalantly for him. Dave knew this was a preplanned action. He also knew he needed to get Pots very quickly because he didn't know how many people were in on this. Pots ruled as school bully so long he might have possessed enough contempt for Dave to act alone. There was one thing Pots had never heard. Dave was the middle weight champion of the academy.

Dave parried the wild right and sent a jab to the face. The jab set up a straight right to the nose. Dave felt bone crunch under the blow. The blow stopped the big man. Digging two lefts to the mid section Dave brought Pots hands down and launched a vicious right hook to Pots cheek. The blow sent the big man to the floor spraying blood from a split in his cheek. Dave hesitated. Perhaps this would be enough.

Pots growled and drew a long bladed knife from his boot. At the crucial point in Pots' rise from the floor Dave kicked him in the ribs. Pots crashed to the floor again and raised his head. Dave sent a boot into the side of Pots head with all the force he could muster.

Pots' limp body rolled to one side. The knife fell out of his hand. Dave picked up the knife and watched Pots inert body. He watched the crowd also. Some of the people who shunned him when he came in were smiling at him now. He saw no threat from the crowd. Pots had been so sure of himself he acted alone. Dave slammed the pointed end of the knife into the hardwood floor beside pots and walked out.

Lesa followed Dave to the car. Vera Lee went to a window to watch.

"You ought to have killed him." Lesa said. "He will try to kill you now. He will have to kill you to save face."

"I may have already done that. I didn't see him move before I left. I kicked him harder than I should have but I didn't know if he was acting alone or if someone else planned to take a hand. I have to go report this fight to my superiors, rules you know." The black car rumbled to life and disappeared down the road.

Lesa watched Dave disappear in a cloud of dust. He's going to call the revenue office she thought. Her thoughts were in a whirl. Her heart had flip flopped when she saw Dave enter the pie supper. She didn't know what to think. Why did she feel sorry for him when Vera Lee snubbed him so coldly? Was he in love with Vera Lee? His face remained a cold mask when Vera Lee snubbed him. Was it this mask that brought her across the floor so quickly? How did she feel about him? What did he think of her? Could he see anymore to her than a school teacher? Somehow she felt there was a hidden knowledge lurking behind the somber gray eyes. Was it because he was looking at her or was it a trait he bestowed on everyone?

Her contact with Dave started as a spy mission. Look the enemy over and exploit his weakness. Could it be anything else? It had been no accident she came to the store when he was there. She wanted a look at him. She'd become far more curious since the Frogville race.

Now she wanted to see him again but not as an enemy. What were her thoughts anyway? Why was she thinking of Dave? How had he gotten into her head? She walked past her car on the way back into the pie supper. Pulling the derringer from her pocket she placed it in the glove box. Pots would never know it, but getting whipped saved his life.

Lesa walked back into the school. Pots was supported by Mr. Harper in a sitting position. He held his bloody face in both hands. Lesa noticed Vera Lee staring out the window in the direction the black car had gone.

Vera Lee knew she had gone too far on the wrong road. How was she going to erase that? Another woman was claiming his attention. She glared at Lesa. What was her involvement in Dave's life and how deep was that involvement? It couldn't be very deep because she'd heard nothing of it. She better do something,

What could she do?

When Lesa returned she heard snatches of conversation. "...Never got a bruise except on his fist ..."

"Never would have believed anyone could do that to old Pots."

"...Should have happened years ago." "Maybe we got Maloy wrong?"

"Pots should have shot that Revenoor ..."

The telephone clicked and crackled in Dave's ear. "And that sir is just about the crop of it." Dave finished the verbal report to the Director.

"Ok we'll send a squad to pick this Pots fellow up. We'll teach him a lesson about pulling a knife on a Federal Agent. Where do we find him?"

"I'd rather you didn't do that sir." Dave was thinking. "Eventually this will have to be settled between me and him."

"Why?" The Director was puzzled. "Isn't this fellow dangerous?"

"Yes he is as dangerous as a loaded shotgun without a safety. I feel my standing with the local people has improved immensely. If you fight my battle for me it will destroy all I've gained."

"Isn't he likely to try to harm you again?" The Director was struggling to understand.

"Oh, he will most definitely be coming after me sooner or later. He has to do it in order to save face with the people. Pots was a bully at school and has lived as a bully ever since. He most likely will try bushwhacking me next time." This was a fact. Dave knew it was going to happen.

"No, I feel there was more behind this fight than just a drunk getting upset over some girl he thinks he's sweet on. Even Pots don't go for blood the way he did. I've been thinking it over all the way in. He came through the door ready to fight. He didn't come in and get worked up over the bidding. The Pie Supper was just an excuse.

"I think Pots may be involved in THE still we're looking for. If he is Joe Joe and Joe Jay Swann are also involved in it. They've gone to ground and quit for now but the pressure is going to build. They will run out of money and the bootleggers are going to run out of whiskey so they will put the pressure on the still operators. They will be making whiskey again. I want Pots on more than an assault charge. When we get him we can toss the assault charge in also." Dave felt like he was running for President after a speech like that one.

"We got people working on this side of the river." The director informed Dave. "If we can coordinate it right we'll make a clean sweep and round up the still operators, the runners, middlemen and the bootleggers all in one bag. We'll get a sealed warrant for Pots. We'll charge him with assault on a police officer with deadly intent. By then we can come up with other charges. If you need to get him out of the way we can unseal the warrant at anytime."

Dave knew what the director was saying. He felt the Director was paying more attention to his advice now than when Dave joined the agency. "Ok, but I'd like to get him on more serious charges than that. If we can catch them at a still maybe we'll be able to find out who burned the barn, feed and poisoned the cows."

"We've received information that indicated there might be a still operating at a place called Bean Creek. Are you familiar with this area?"

"Yes sir, I walked the full length of Bean Creek a few days ago. Someone might have seen me and decided it would be a safe place since I'd already searched it and found nothing. I'll go check it again."

Pots fingered the swollen crooked nose and

crossed his eyes trying to look directly at it. He didn't like what the mirror showed him. He tipped the mirror to show the split cheek and permanently cauliflowered ear. *"How did this happen to me?"* He mumbled to himself. *"I've whipped everyone I fought since I was in the third grade. I made them all step lively. When we were in school I whipped that punk Miloy anytime I felt like doing it. How did he whip me this time and do it so quickly in front of so many people?*

He hit me before I was ready. That's it! He sneaked a punch in when I wasn't expecting it. Then he kicked me while I was down. I'll whip anyone who says different." Pots slammed his fist into the wall. He grabbed at his sore ribs and groaned. "I'll kill that SOB. I was going to kill him for business reasons. Now I'm going to kill him for personal reasons."

CHAPTER 8

Vera Lee seemed to do her best thinking in front of a mirror arranging her hair. She rearranged her hair again and again. She rose and wandered restless around the room. She remained convinced Dave would come back. She had known he was back in the valley but he'd not called on her. She'd spent hours waiting for the rumble of an engine and cloud of dust to announce his arrival.

When Jack barked and she looked out the window her heart did a flip flop. Dave was back! Her hair! Her dress? How could she let him catch her in such a mess? Tossing caution to the wind she was about to rush out when she saw her father approaching the gate.

Her excitement died when she realized Dave was driving an agency truck and had a badge on his chest. Why did he have to do this? Could he not see? He was an outcast and if she married him she would be in the same boat. She was the queen bee in the valley. If she married him she would share his fate. She could not, she would not do this.

Of all the nerve! She'd given him a choice between her and the Agency. He'd chosen the Agency. Never in her wildest dreams did she believe he would choose the Agency. Once the words were out, her pride wouldn't let her take them back. Besides, if she stood firm he would come to his senses and realize what he was losing and crawl apologetically back.

For his second trip up Bean Creek Dave drove an agency pickup truck. He had a good chuckle when he signed the truck out. The truck was supposed to look like any farmer Brown truck. It was light blue. The gun rack in the back window was decorated with a hot shot and lariat rope. There were two bales of hay and a pair of worn out chaps in the bed. Dave almost looked for the blue heeler cow dog. The truck was just the right amount of dirty. They had taken the state license plate off and replaced it with a commercial plate. Evidently the person who did the makeup work on the truck didn't know the people of the valley either had no license tags at all or had farm tags. It really didn't really matter but the folks in the valley would have the truck spotted from a mile away. It might be good to furnish them with a chuckle now and then.

It was a glorious day. Dave sat in the truck with the door open and watched a bird building a nest in a hollow Oak. There is a part and place for everything in nature. Here a mortally wounded tree helped bring new life into the world. There were claw marks on the bark and the opening around the hole was worn smooth. The tree furnished a raccoon a snug warm bed during the cold days of winter.

There is no waste in nature. When the tree comes to the end of its life it will fall and decay. It will melt slowly into the humus and feed the new life springing up to fill the void its death left in the cover of the world.

Dave took his time. He thought this was a long hike that wasn't necessary. He didn't really mind going. The hike was nothing for him and the world was coming to life around him. Dogwoods were fading and new growth was springing up everywhere. A carpet of flowers covered every open spot in the forest.

He couldn't help but look for the Cottonmouth under the rock. If it had been a little earlier he might have seen it. There was a Cottonmouth den under the rock. They came out to enjoy the sun on warm days in early spring. At this late date they were dispersing to their respective feed grounds.

While he was bent to look under the rock he smelled it. The faintest odor of wood smoke went past on the quiet breeze. Circling around sniffing like a hound dog searching for the scent of game Dave could smell smoke occasionally. Normally in mountain country the air moves uphill during daylight hours and downhill at night. Dave didn't know if he could trust this today. As light as the breeze was today it could be coming from anywhere. He stuck his finger in his mouth and held it up. The breeze was moving downhill.

Climbing up the side of the mountain, he eased into a small side canyon. The scent got stronger and he could smell the mash. A small tendril of smoke rose above the timber up stream from where he was. He moved in that direction.

Dave knew he should back out and call for back-up. Again he was like a hound dog. He had game in sight and he was going to at least look down on the still before he left.

Coming around the mountain he crept behind a boulder. A bush grew in front of the boulder and furnished a screen that would break up his outline and conceal the movement when he peeked over the boulder.

There was only one man working the still. He was a long tall skinny man with brown hair that was long and floppy for the day. Dave watched the man.

He didn't recognize him. Where did he come from? He wasn't one of the valley residents. His Farmer John overalls showed in stark contrast as he stooped to pour the results of the drip into a jug.

Dave made himself comfortable and watched while the sun crept from brunch to lunch. He saw no one else. He saw no other movement. This fellow was running the still alone. The sun was so warm and comfortable he dozed. The sound of the ax woke him. The bootlegger was preparing wood for the firebox.

He knew policy was not to raid a still with less than two agents and preferably more than that. It was for the Agent's protection. If anything happened there would be two to shoot or testify. Dave studied the terrain. If he went back to the trail a hump would shield his approach until he was fairly close. If the man stayed where he was a big Yellow Pine would cover Dave until he got real close to the still.

Dave quietly withdrew around the shoulder of the mountain. Coming off the mountain he turned up stream toward the still. Being very careful not to roll a rock or break a twig. He peeked over the hump. The fellow was still in the same place. He eased over behind the pine until he was close enough to touch it. The man was still in the same place. His back turned toward Dave.

Dave took his badge and ID out and held it in his left hand. He loosed the snap on his service revolver and stepped from behind the tree. He'd only taken a step or two when the man spun around. One of his long arms instinctively grabbed the ever present lever action rifle.

"Hold it! Freeze where you are!" Dave held the badge and ID high. "Federal Agent! Put it down!"

The man looked at Dave then began surveying the woods trying to locate other Revenoors.

"Put it down!" Dave repeated himself.

The man turned slowly around looking at the woods. Dave watched closely. He was prepared to act if the fellow took the rifle in the other hand or raised it. The man pivoted until his back was toward Dave. Looking over his shoulder the man smiled a slow smile, and then leaped up the trail at a star-tling rate of speed. Dave stood for a startled second. He couldn't shoot this man in the back. Besides it wouldn't be wise to start a shoot out from this dis-tance. He held a handgun and the adversary pos-sessed a rifle.

"Stop!" Dave ordered leaping up the trail af-ter the man. He had no doubts about his ability to catch the fleeing man. Dave excelled at cross coun-try running. In the past he'd won a string of mara-thon events. It felt good to stretch out. "You better run sucker," he yelled at the back in front of him. Dave watched his footing. They were running on rough uneven ground across the woods. He pound-ed on with an uneven stride. His feet missed most of the rocks. Leaping over a downed log he blew a hole in the briars and brambles. At first he gained a little but since then the back stayed about the same distance ahead of him.

The chase came out the head of Bean Creek. They ran through a big gap and turned down the long ridges leading to East Creek. Dave felt good.

His breathing came in long easy puffs. This dude ought to start running out of gas soon. Dave loved running downhill. It was one of his strong points. He'd catch this fellow now. When he caught this fellow he was going to tackle him and enjoy doing it. He put on more speed. The back stayed the same distance ahead.

The chase crossed East Creek. Dave's breathing became labored. Who was this tall galoot in the overalls? Were did he come from anyway? What was he doing making whiskey in these hills? He didn't live in the valley. Dave was sure of that.

They turned up Grassy Ridge. Dave was breathing hard now. The back was about the same distance in front of him. He'd gained nothing.

The chase continued across Walls Rough Canyon and climbed Cabin Mountain. Dave's stride became unsteady. Cramps ran up and down his thighs. His lungs burned and his breath came in ragged gasps. The heavy boots were taking their toll. He locked his eyes on the back in front of him and let his will drive him on. The back was so close. If he could gain just a few more feet he could grab a collar and end this. He staggered on.

When they hit the top of Cabin Mountain Dave knew it was now or never. He turned on the last of his reserves. He gained a step or two. The runner looked back and increased his speed to match Dave's. The chase was going down the relative flat top of Cabin Mountain. Dave's foot hit a loose rock and it rolled under his foot. His legs were too tired and cramped to compensate for the rolling stone.

Dave fell heavily. His shoulder took the first part of the blow. He rolled to his back and then over to his stomach. Dave lay stunned for a moment. He rolled to his back and sat up; his breath came in long ragged gasps.

"Fellow are you alright?" Startled Dave looked up. The man he'd been chasing was just out of his reach looking into his eyes. The man was resting on one knee holding his rifle by the barrel with the butt on the ground. His cheek rested on the hand holding the rifle barrel. His breathing was heavy but even. Dave started to rise. The man backed a step or two. Dave stuck his hand out as if asking for a hand up.

"Pashaw!" The man snorted. "You laying there on the ground unconscious is one thing and you awake and all grabby is another." The man walked a few feet away and sat on a rock.

Dave seated himself on the closest rock. "Who are you?" He asked.

The man smiled. "My name is Body, N.O. Body." He chuckled at his own joke.

Dave tried to figure a way to catch this man. He couldn't come up with any kind of workable plan. He still had his service revolver. He wasn't about to start a shoot out with this fellow. Not shaking like he was now anyway. He wished he didn't have the revolver. The pistol felt like it weighed a ton. Due to good conditioning Dave recovered quickly. The boots blistered his feet. He considered taking them off and decided against it.

Dave leaped off the rock and lunged at the guy. The man came from a sitting position and hit full stride in two jumps. The chase came down the top of the mountain. At the center of the mountain it turned north down the rough ridges leading to Black Fork Creek. Dave put his all into the five miles of downhill to the creek but the fellow stayed the same distance ahead.

When Dave crossed the creek a cramp hit him in the side and brought him to a screeching halt. Bent over breathing deeply, he swung his arm in a circle. The cramp subsided. He seated himself on a log and retched, then again. The man took a seat on another log watching Dave closely. Who was this guy anyway? Dave studied his face. I ought to know a man who can run like this, he thought. Again Dave racked his brain as to how could he get his hands on this jasper. He could think of no way. He'd chase him again and hope the fellow would trip and fall or something.

Dave leaped off the log. When he looked up the man wasn't running. He was standing straddle legged with the rifle in one hand and held the other hand palm out toward Dave. "Stop!" He ordered.

Without thinking Dave stopped.

"Enough for today," the man said. "Do you know your way back? Can you go home from here?" The man seemed sincerely concerned.

Dave looked around and dumbly shook his head.

"It's been fun. We'll have to do it again sometime." The hand moved up and down with a bye bye wave and the man disappeared through the briars like a bad memory.

Dave hobbled to the creek. He sat on a rock and removed his socks. They were crusted with dried blood. His poor feet sported blisters on top of blisters. His feet were swollen until his toes separated like fat sausages. Easing both his burning, stinging feet into the cold clear water of the creek felt so good he let out a grunt of satisfaction. Dave carefully washed the blood out of his socks and hung them on a bush to dry. Breaking a half inch piece of a twig, he flicked it out on the water. A big splash resulted when a big perch slashed from his nest under the bank and smacked the bit of twig.

The cramps and knots began to smooth out and dissipate. His breathing returned to normal.

The cold water reduced the swelling in his feet. He was feeling better but not much better because he lost the race. He ran the lean frame, long face and straight brown hair back and forth though his memory banks. He could remember no one who fit the description. He lay back to think it over. It was down right embarrassing to be outrun as easily as he had been. He realized he'd never really been in the race. The man was carrying him along to keep him running. The waiting at the rest stops had been to get him to continue on, the old mama bird trick. She would act hurt and flutter around to lead the fox or coyote away from her nest.

Dave sat bolt up right. That still would be gone before he got back to it! He knew it would be gone. All his evidence would be long gone. Sore muscles, aching feet and a little education were all he'd get out of this round. Not having a prisoner or evidence was more paperwork than it would be if he came in with both in tow. How long was it going to take him to get this revenue thing down?

Even if he had caught the guy all the evidence

would be gone and the race would have been for nothing. He decided that since he'd broken standard operating procedure and lost everything he wouldn't report this one.

CHAPTER 9

Vera Lee sat in front of the mirror arranging and rearranging her hair again. Dave ignored her! She snubbed him but he should have pursued her. He could have followed her and made some effort to get back into her good graces. *I am the reason he came back. I'm the reason he came to the Pie Supper. Give him time. He will come to me.* Vera Lee struggled to convince herself.

He would have chased me if that Lesa hadn't interfered. Lesa zeroed in on Dave like the striking snake she is. Why did Dave have to be so stubborn? If he begged in the right manner I might marry him anyway.

Now he had another woman circling him like

a buzzard. Dave ignored her pie and bid an outrageous price for Lesa's. *Of course he couldn't be interested in Lesa while I'm around. He'd just used the bid to get at me and make Pots mad. What is that mousy Lesa up to anyway? Everyone knows Dave belongs to me.* She tried to think of something she could use to get him looking at her and her only. She was sure she could explain the snubs away.

Vera Lee slapped the dresser with the brush and paced impatiently to the window.

She drew the curtain back and stared at the gate. In her mind's eye she could see Dave kneeling in front of old Dan. She thought of Dave's gentle hands caressing the old dogs head.

The curtains fell into place and she paced restlessly around the room. Why didn't she run into Dave's arms then? Her father would have been upset. She couldn't stand the stigma of being a Revenoor's wife although she could sense a change in some people's opinion after the pie supper. If she hadn't been so upset and ran out she could have helped form some of the opinions. *If I had been inside ...?*

Whoa! Perhaps I've been going about this wrong. I have to get back inside Dave's life. When I get back inside his life I will persuade him to leave the Revenue Service. How can I get Dave to dump that Lesa and look at me? Vera Lee turned the lights off and sauntered down the stairs.

Pots roared long and loud about Dave's sneaky ways. Hit a man before he was ready. Pots knew in his heart of hearts he was the one who threw the sucker punch and had been beaten by superior skill. He sure didn't want a repeat of the fight. No way! He would do it in a different way next time.

Joe Joe and Joe Ray became silent and moody. The banter died out of them. They were tired of listening to the lie, but neither wanted trouble with Pots. All three of them fell deeper into the product they sold.

George Coldfield made whiskey since the days of the great depression. In those dark and dreary days there was no work or money for anything. George's wife came down with a case of pneumonia. George had no money for medicine. He ran his first batch of moonshine to pay for the medicine that kept her alive. George continued to make whiskey after that fateful day. He'd developed a market far to the north. He wouldn't sell a drop to the local drunks.

George was a medium built man, whose hair line crept backward every year. The brown eyes and wind tanned face always had an amused look about them. Laughter came easy to him. He saw the world and was amused by the workings of it. George could, and did, make the best sipping whiskey in the business. He had a standing order of so many gallons per month. George and Nita Colman were teetotalers. They never sampled the produce of George's still. Whiskey was to be sold not drank.

Over the years George developed a good herd of pure bred cattle. He bred the best Brahma bulls in the business. He also raised a few hogs.

Nita Colman was a neat wiry grandmotherly type of woman. Her skirts swept the floor. An apron with a bib was nearly as long as the skirt. A row of pockets wound around the waist of the apron. Her waist length gray streaked brown hair was done up in a tidy bun at the nape of her neck. An old fashioned bonnet hung handy to hand beside the back door.

Nita cooked their meals on a home comfort wood burning cook stove. She was head cook, dish washer, clothes washer, housekeeper and gardener. All the water for this came from a well and was drawn by hand. She raised a garden and preserved the produce. Mostly by drying or canning. Nita maintained a good supply of jams and jellies. There was the cow to milk, the chickens, baby and grown, to tend and eggs to gather.

Anything Nita needed or wanted came from Sears & Roebuck, Montgomery Ward or she made it herself. A truck brought such food and supplies as they ordered once a month. The fact that she sometimes saw another woman only once a year didn't bother Nita one bit. She didn't have time for, or listening to gossip. She did cook for and listen to the stockmen and hunters that occasionally passed through the hills.

The Colman place was located deep in the mountains. They moved in when land could be had for paying a small amount of taxes due on it. Thanks to George's whiskey still they were able to raise enough money to claim a considerable amount of acres.

The sloping ridges and small canyons were covered with various kinds of Oaks, Hickory, and huge Yellow Pine. Various species of other trees filled in between. The four to six foot through Yellow Pine towered over all other trees in the area. Shin high Summer Huckleberry bushes grew in profusion under the Pines. Plentiful creeks and springs watered this area year around.

Colman situated his house in a "gap" where two mountains came together forming a large flat spot. He located his house on one side of the old Government road and the barn on the other side. This way the run off water from the house and barn ran down opposite sides of the mountain. Behind the house he built a smoke house.

Cliff Cooper and Roy Freeman were the village drunks. If a liquid contained any form of alcohol they drank it. Neither had the get up and go to operate a still. They were always together. If you saw one you saw the other.

They sat on the porch. The Sun's shadow sneaked silently across the porch and neither wanted to spend the energy it took to move to the other end. They lost a fierce and protracted battle to John Barley Corn last night and the hangover was burning fiercely. John Barley Corn's body lay by Cliff's feet with a cork driven into it so not even the smell could get away. "We've got to do something." Cliff cast a doleful eye on the small amount of whiskey rolling around in the bottom of the jug. "We have to have a hair of the dog."

"Where's the other Jug?" Roy questioned.

"We drank it." Cliff tossed off the small amount in the jug.

"It was my turn! You drank out of turn!" Roy grabbed the jug and stared down the small opening with one eye closed.

Cliff turned his pockets wrong side out and looked at Roy. "Do you have any money?"

"You know I don't have any money. It was my money that bought the jug you just killed." Roy cast accusing eyes on Cliff.

"Where could we get whiskey on the credit?" Cliff was already thinking of the shakes.

"I don't know. We owe everybody in the country and that sorry Dave Miloy has shut most of the stills down. The ones he didn't catch quit making." It was looking bleak to Roy.

"Do you have anything we can sell to get a jug?" Cliff looked around at their few belongings.

"Tomorrow is livestock sale day. We'll have to catch some wild hogs and take them to the sale. You know, you might consider selling Butch. He's the best hog dog in the country. I bet we could get three or four jugs for him."

Cliff drew himself up full height. "Sell Butch? Sell Butch? You would kill the goose that lay the golden egg? Butch has gotten us more jugs than anything else!"

"Yeah, I guess you're right. As long as he can't tell a wild hog from someone's pet hog we better keep him."

"Where could we go? Charlie Winters said he'd

shoot us if we came back on his range. The old Coot is crazy enough to do it too. I'm not going over there." Cliff cast around.

"We went to John's range last time. Let's go to George Colman's stomping grounds, but let's be sure we don't get any of his hogs. I'm not sure of what he'd do. He might shoot and the least he'd do was ban us from that part of the country. It's a good thing this is open range country or we would have no place to go." Roy was working it out.

The Sun had not reached its zenith when the pair stole enough gasoline from a county tractor at the rock pit to get up into the Colman area. The county had been a reliable source of fuel for years. They never took it all. They would go several days in a row rather than stir the workers up over the missing gasoline.

The sun bore hard on the old Chevy truck puttering down the rocky dirt road. Cliff dodged the larger rocks here and there.

"Whoa!" Roy commanded pointing to tracks in the road.

Cliff obediently obeyed. Roy leaped from the passenger's seat bumping the rifle barrel on the door and slowly walked down the road. "These tracks are fresh. Two sows and both have pigs with them. We're out here in the edge of no man's land. We ought to be able to get both the sows and their pigs."

"See if we can get the pickup behind that thicket of little pines. I don't want it sitting in plain sight." Cliff was worried.

Roy walked behind the little pines watching the ground for obstacles that might stop the truck. He was almost on it before he looked up. There it sat, an oak barrel. He pushed on it. It was full. He immediately looked around. There was no one in sight. He walked a bigger circle. He saw no one.

It was a barrel like they shipped whiskey in but he couldn't believe there was a whole barrel of whisky sitting here unattended. No one would do that. He tried to pull the bung to see what the contents were. It most likely was a barrel of water. The bung was driven in so tight he couldn't shake it with his bare hand. Returning to the truck he fished a screwdriver out of the tool box.

"What is it? What are you doing?" Cliff was puzzled.

"You wouldn't believe it if I told you." Roy walked away. Cliff opened the door and followed him.

Roy carefully pried the bung from the barrel. The smell of good corn whiskey permeated the air. "Ahhh," Roy breathed the fumes in. A whole barrel of whiskey, an ocean of whiskey! "They surely wouldn't mind us taking a drink."

"How can we get it out of the barrel?" Cliff was a step ahead of Roy.

"We have the hose we siphoned the gas with." Roy was already walking toward the pickup.

"Blow through it and that will take most of the gas out of it." Cliff was bent over smelling the aroma rising through the bung hole.

Poking one end the hose into the barrel the pair sat on the ground and leaned back against the barrel. Roy sucked on the hose and put his thumb over the end to stop the flow. "Tastes like gas," he said passing the hose to Cliff.

"Sure does." Cliff wiped his mouth with the back of his hand. "It sure is good though."

Roy passed the hose to Cliff for the fourth time. "The gas taste is gone." He remarked. "You left the jug sitting on the stump at home. How are we going to get some of this home? The fellow who made this whiskey surely wouldn't mind us taking a jug with us."

Cliff took another hit off the hose. "Why take a jug when we can have the whole barrel? Nobody knows we're up here."

"Yeah, nobody should leave a whole barrel of whiskey unattended. Serve them right." The mounting level of alcohol in their blood opened the way for poor judgment.

Cliff backed the truck into a ditch. After driving the bung solidly into the hole they rolled the barrel into the back of the truck.

Roy tied both their jackets around the barrel in an effort to disguise it. They arrived at Roy's house and lay two boards from the truck to the porch and rolled the barrel onto the porch. Carefully filling the jug they'd left on the stump, they began to celebrate their unbelievable find.

George sopped his plate and ate the last piece of the biscuit before he rose from the supper table. "It will be dark soon. I've got to meet the boys. I'll be back shortly. We have three barrels that are to be transported north tonight. These barrels will to be buried inside a load of baled hay on Slim's truck.

George saddled old Baldy and rode into long shadows of the setting sun. He noted the tracks in the road before he reached the pine thicket. The tracks were as plain to him as a signature. He knew the footprints of every vehicle that moved in his part of the world. It was his business. This was an easy one. Roy and Cliff picked up tires anywhere they could find them. They weren't about to spend good drinking money on tires. The track had four different treads with the right front being a little wider than the rest. He knew the barrel was gone before he looked behind the thicket of pines.

He saw where the tracks turned and went back

out. The other barrels remained where he left them. He could make up the short fall on the load. He'd have to wait for the truck before he went after the missing barrel.

Riding into the house well after dark he apprised Nita of the situation. She rolled some cold biscuits, a jar of canned venison and coffee. She dropped these into his saddle bags with a, "be careful now," she closed the door.

It was a beautiful sunrise. The colors seemed to explode across the sky. The leaves of the big oak and the corner of the porch framed it perfectly. George sat in a chair tipped back against the wall sipping his coffee. He watched the sleeping pair with that quaint smile of his. They were both sprawled on the porch. Neither was able to get inside before they passed out.

Roy flailed around and rose to a sitting position. He rubbed his head and looked fuzzily around. The click of the shotgun hammer being drawn back caught his attention. His eyes focused on George. "No! God no!" He threw an arm up protect his face.

The scream woke Cliff. He sat up groggily. The other hammer on the double barrel came clicking back. Both men were instantly sober. Both waited for the hail of buckshot that would end their lives. George sat and smiled at them.

"There's a cup of coffee sitting beside you. Drink it!" The smile played around George's mouth. Both men drank the coffee at a gulp. "Pour another from the pot on the edge of the porch and drink it slowly. I want both of you cold sober."

"Mr. Colman I don't think I could be more sober than I am right now."

"All the way over here I had it in mind to kill both of you thieving skunks. I walked in here and found the two of you lying in your own puke, soiling your clothes and stinking worse than a hog pen. I decided killing you would be doing you a kindness. The worst thing I could do to you was to let you live. This porch stinks worse than a dead cow. Feel of your throats!" Each man placed a hand to his throat. It came away bloody. They looked at their shirts. The fronts of the shirts were soaked in blood.

"While you were passed out I cut both your throats. I didn't cut them deep enough to kill you. I cut them just enough to let you know I wouldn't have needed to waste gunpowder on you. There will be a scar to remind you to never set foot in the north mountains again." George rose and pointed at the barrel. "I've measured the barrel. Don't you dare take another drink out of it! I will give you what you have already drank. The barrel will be back where you got it by the time I ride home."

"If I hear or even suspicion you of turning me in, or getting any kind of word to Miloy, may God rest your souls. The rest of you will be mine." George deliberately turned his back and walked out the gate. His entire being was concentrated in his ears. He hoped to hear the scrape of a rifle being picked up. He was offering them the chance. He felt he was making a mistake leaving this pair of vermin alive. Cliff and Roy sat very still until George mounted and rode off. Never had they been closer to meeting their maker than they were a few minutes ago.

The barrel was in the appointed place when

George arrived. He pulled the bung and tipped the barrel over. He watched the whiskey soak into the soil. The gasoline ruined the barrel as well as the whiskey in it.

Back at headquarters the Director sat in his comfortable chair and watched the Agents squirm in their uncomfortable seats. "There is a rumor the bootleggers are stealing from each other."

"A couple of the worse drunks in the country stole a barrel of whiskey from a still operator." Dave said off handedly.

"You know who the still operator is and you haven't arrested him?" The director swelled in his chair.

"We don't have any evidence yet." Dave was relaxed. "His time will come."

"I think his time should have come when you learned he was making whiskey!" The director leaned his forearms on his desk.

"What evidence do we have? A sigh off the backwoods telegraph? Some of the people are starting to accept me. They're becoming convinced the country would be better off without the stills. I'm hearing things again. There is no bootlegger up there worth damaging this fragile start." Dave was fully alert now.

"I think we should try to corral this fellow." The director couldn't let go.

"We've shut down enough stills and put enough people in jail to get the Governor off your back. That big still is about due to fire up again soon and if we are diverted they will have the Governor on the war path again." Dave reasoned.

"Who do you think has the whiskey?" Harold questioned.

"I think it is George Colman."

"The rancher?"

"None other. You see there are no secrets in the valley. There are too few people and they are too close together. Information flows with the wind. You fellows will never hear it but it is there." Dave was wondering where this conversation was going.

"Where do you think the Colman whiskey is going?" Chester questioned.

"North, I don't know where yet. Look, we need to concentrate on the booze crossing the river south. After we shut it down we can branch out." Dave was getting worked up.

"I know the Colman place. There is the house and a smokehouse behind it. That smokehouse would be good place to stash a barrel of whiskey you'd just picked up." Harold said.

"I think we should pursue it." The director had his fingers steepled on his desk.

"How could you find out if George has whiskey in the smokehouse? We don't have enough evidence to get a search warrant. There is no use bothering with it if he doesn't have any whiskey. All we'd be doing was put him on full alert. He'd know we were after him and he might go to ground like the southern still and we'd be left waiting again." Dave argued.

"We could send someone to look." The director suggested.

"Not me!" Harold turned white.

"How about you Dave?"

"Why don't we try to get a search warrant? If George has anything we can find it and arrest him legally."

The Director leaned back in his chair thoughtfully. He looked at the ceiling for a long moment. "I don't think so. Even old Judge Gray wouldn't give us a search warrant on the information we have."

"I tell you we are looking at another Charlie Winter's situation. We didn't come out of that one looking or feeling too good. Let's wait and set it up later. The still running whiskey south should start up again any day now. It is the one bugging the Goverener." Dave reasoned.

"I remember you promised to arrest Charlie Winters, which you haven't accomplished yet. Dave you arrest George and take him out of the house. With George gone Chester could safely look in the smokehouse for the whiskey."

"I will get Charlie Winters. He's small potatoes. He sells very little whiskey and that goes to local people. There is no use in him or some us dying trying to arrest him. I guarantee you this can happen very easily. You barrel in there trying to slap iron on Charlie and it will be worse than going after a grizzly in a cave. On his own ground, that old man is meaner than a bobcat in a hole. He's fast as a falcon and sly as a fox. He grew up in those mountains. He's been there and did that. The right time will come.

"I will arrest George Colman. What do I charge him with? I want to go on record as opposing this George Coldman operation." Dave was operating against his better judgment.

CHAPTER 10

The sun was low in the western sky. Its filtered light cast long shadows across the playground. The children burst through the door in a screaming mass. The boys raced down the road in a burst of joy to be living. The girls followed with their heads together sharing secrets.

Vera Lee stepped aside and let the last child out the schoolhouse door before she entered it. Lesa sat behind her desk putting papers in order to be graded.

"Hello," Vera Lee floated up the aisle from the door.

Lesa looked up and placed the papers aside.

"Hello." Lesa leaned back. This was an unexpected visitor.

"I only have a moment. I wanted to thank you for your help at the pie supper and invite you to a sewing bee the ladies are having at my house this weekend." Vera Lee stopped beside Lesa's desk.

"Yes, I believe we had a better pie supper this time than ever before." Lesa emphasized the "we". "Thanks to the generous bids we made more money out of it than ever before."

The corners of Vera Lee's eyes tightened. Her grip on the small bag was fierce. "This room brings back so many memories," she gushed. "I used to sit right here," she walked to a desk and sat down. "Dave Miloy sat behind me. He was such a pain. He was so impulsive. Always pestering me," she toyed with her hair. "Of course I always ignored him."

"It seems to have become a habit." Lesa clasped her hands and laid them on the desk in front of her.

Again Vera Lee's eyes tightened but she maintained control. "Dave has always been impulsive. Since he was small he'd try something new but he really is a fundamental type guy who always returns to the basics."

"Of course you have known him longer than I have but it seems to me like he is a solid man. He is a man who sees what he wants and goes after it. If anyone in this valley could have stopped him that Internal Revenue Service Badge wouldn't be pinned on his shirt."

The Bitch! Thought Vera Lee. *When I have Dave safely back in my fold I will fry her and run her out of the country!* She fought hard and maintained control. "I must be going. Remember the sewing bee. We must see more of each other."

"I'm sure we will." Lizzy's eyes were gleaming out of Lesa's face.

Lesa sat still after Vera Lee left. *Be careful* she warned herself. *You are still an outsider. You have won the people of the valley over but in a show down with Vera Lee you will still be an outsider. It could very well cost you your livelihood. Am I ready to stake this to see Dave? Did Dave really know she was alive or was she just another one of those people Dave was aware of but didn't want to know any further?*

Why am I spending so much time thinking about Dave? The most important and central thought in her mind was what would Dave think of the Ford snuggled down in the barn across the road. If, or perhaps it was just when, he found it.

She sat in a maze of indecision. She became aware of the throaty rumble of a big engine coming up the road. Her heart leaped. There were only two engines of that class in the country. And she knew where one of them was.

The rumble died off and the engine grumbled its way to the door. The engine was revved to a high RPM then dropped suddenly. The back rap shook the windows until engine faded to a stop. The silence was shattering when the engine died.

Unmoved Lesa sat behind her desk. A hat sailed through the open door. A long silence, a head peeped around the door jam. "Teacher I'm sorry I'm late."

"Actually you are a bit tardy." Lesa thought of Vera Lee's visit.

Dave walked to his old seat and sat down. "I sat in this seat for eight years," he said.

"So I have been told, and all eight of those years you pestered the girl seated in front of you."

"Well, you know how boys are."

"Yes, they call it the language of love. I've also seen the big heart carved in that desk with the words VERA LEE across it."

Dave was silent for a long moment. "Isn't it too bad that we can't stay in that first love stage forever? Why do we have to wake up and face the world?" Dave shifted gears. "What I really stopped for was the Steak House over on the Stateline has a big steak with my name on it and I need someone to help me salt it. How about it?"

Lesa's heart froze. Here it was. The decision had to be made. She was terrified.

This was it, a fork in the road of life. No matter what she did or did not do her life was changed forever. Did she take the safe road or toss everything to the wind and follow her heart? Did she hunker down and exist on the comfortable road or did she roll the dice and hope she could live over it?

"Well," Dave said misreading the look on her face, "I didn't mean to insult you. I realize eating with me will make you very unpopular with some of the people. Some might say you are getting information from the kids and passing it on to me. I'll understand if you don't want to face that."

"No, no," Lesa decided quickly when the shadow of disappointment settled on Dave's face. "Do you think this steak would keep long enough for a person to shower and get dressed?"

Dave spun out of the chair. "See you in two hours!" He leaped out the door.

The meal was better than she ever could have dreamed it would be. The food was good and the easy chatter back and forth was relaxing and informative. She was getting an insight into Dave's past life.

They discussed powerful, fast cars and what it took to make a car fast and which make of stock car was the fastest. Dave was sure Lesa knew more than she was telling. The dust filled, engine roaring chase at Frogville came into his mind. The corner where he almost had the runner still bothered him. He missed the chance to end the chase in his favor and it'd been the only chance he got. Perhaps getting outrun was what annoyed him most.

It'd been a long time since Dave spent time around someone he could relax with. He'd been so tied up with the Academy and whiskey still wars it was unbelievably comfortable to sit back, chatter and laugh about nothing in particular.

On the way home Dave withdrew into himself. He slowly settled into himself.

"What have I did or said?" Lesa asked herself as she searched frantically for any indiscretion.

."I'm sorry to bring you home this early and breakup an evening I've enjoyed so much." Dave cast a worried look at her. "But duty calls."

Dave sat with the headlights on while Lesa floated through the door on Fairy wings.

He crowded the black car hard on his way back to pick up the agency truck. Speed always seemed to sharpen his thinking.

Dave's headlights flashed along the corral fence and lit the brand on the barn door as he swung around into the front gate of George Colman's house. A bunch of pigs bedded along the fence spooked and went whooshing and squealing down the hill beside the barn. Two stock dogs and an old hound ran barking and nipping at the wheels. A flock Guinea hens roosting in the corner of the yard set up a pot-racking noise that could be heard a mile away. A turkey gobbled from the ridge pole of the barn. The horses stirred restlessly in the corral.

When were the city folks going to learn it was nigh onto impossible to sneak up on one of these hillbilly homesteads? Any one of these things and more would tip these people off to a stranger being in the vicinity. Even the Whippoorwills sitting in the dust of the road would send a warning.

George stood framed in the door. He'd been listening to Dave's progress on the way in for sometime. He remained impassive. He recognized the trucks exhaust sound before he saw it. Dave clicked the yard gate open.

"Mr. Colman? It's Dave Miloy. I have a warrant for your arrest." Dave stopped to let this soak in.

Colman stood unmoved for a moment. "What is the warrant for?" He knew he should have stuck Cliff and Roy like a couple of slaughter hogs. It would have been so easy. This was an oversight that could be corrected.

"Manufacturing and delivering alcoholic beverages the taxes have not been paid on." Dave was patient. He waited for George to digest and analyze the situation.

Another protracted moment. Colman looked at Nita. "Ok," he said and reached up over the door.

"Hold it!" Dave adamantly ordered.

Colman stopped.

"When that hand comes back down it better have nothing but a hat in it."

Colman smiled the gentle smile and lowered the hat enough for Dave to see and pushed through the door.

Dave held a pair of handcuffs out. "I don't like

to do this but it is required of me. Put your hands out in front"

Colman walked through the gate in front of Dave. Dave was walking somewhat sideways. He didn't expect Nita to take this quietly and he knew her ability with a rifle. George walked to the truck door and stood beside it. Dave assisted him into the cab.

Dave drove up the hill a half mile from the house and shut the engine off.

"What's going on?" George demanded. He was puzzled.

"We're just waiting on a fellow. He is supposed to meet us here."

They sat silent and watched the ghostly shadows the wind caressed tree limbs and bright moonlight created. The warm, balmy moonlit night cast a spell on them. Both were soaked in their own thoughts. Dave was wondering about Lesa's other life. Where had she been before she moved here? Why did she come to such a poor place as the valley to teach school?

"Mr. Colman, this didn't come from me. Cliff & Roy didn't report you." Dave ventured tentatively. "Perhaps I can save you some trouble there."

"If they didn't tell you, how did you know I had any contact with them?"

"You know the backwoods telegraph. There are no real secrets in the valley." Dave leaned back and relaxed. "There had to be an explanation as to how they both had the same brand on their throats."

"Don't you feel bad coming back and harassing your own people?" George wasn't fussing, he had a genuine interest.

Dave considered it carefully. "I didn't want to come back at first but it was required of me. I've spent a lot of time covering most of the valley. The main export from this valley is its young people. Booze is secondary. When a young person gets old enough and needs to make a living they have to leave the valley. There is very little work here. This valley is one hundred years behind the rest of the nation.

"The days of the moonshiner are over. The

Governments of the country the customers live in have decided to stop the traffic. If we can't stop it the Governor will send the National Guard in. If I know these people, there would be major causalities on both sides." Dave was silent for a long moment.

"I've decided that what I do is going to help the country in the long run. We'll shut the stills down and clean the country up. Perhaps if we go about it right we can move the country out of the old feud set of mind and get some kind of industry in here. If the people of this valley would work together we might accomplish something." Dave was silent and George looked at him.

"I know I'm a dreamer but I plan to stay in this part of the country and do what I can."

Chester was proud of himself; he'd made it to the smoke house door without being detected by any of the animals. He reached up and took hold of the latch. A quick peek and he'd be on his way. KER-POW! The muzzle blast hurt his ears. The latch in his hand disintegrated when the one hundred eighty grain silver tip bullet hit it. The shock waves set up by the big bullet striking the latch numbed his arm all the way to the shoulder. He thought he'd been hit.

Chester ran around the smokehouse and headed for the relative safety of the woods. He stumped his toe and rolled over the rocks. KER-POW! The bullet stripped the bark off a tree beside him, tiny pieces of lead and bark burned his face, arms, and neck. Chester totally panicked. He wanted to be someplace that rifle wasn't. He ran full speed in the moonlight. Chester's hand pulled the service revolver from its holster. He would …. The dark body of a tree loomed up one step before he hit it. He saw a bright flash of light and then blackness when he hit the tree.

Chester rolled to a stop on his back. Nita walked to his body and looked at him. He was breathing. Blood was flowing from the broken nose. Nita knew she had not hit him. She was a past master with a rifle. Every bullet went where she told it to.

"Durn Revenuers." She said. "Who do they think they are, invading a body's privacy this way?" Nita backed up the trail a few steps and waited.

Chester rolled groggily to his hands and knees and looked for the revolver. KER-POW the dirt and gravel leaped into his face again. Tiny bits of lead and rocks sent a firestorm rippling down the side of his face and body. Chester staggered a few steps and fell again. Nita watched him for few moments. He was staggering blindly down the hill. Turning back toward the house, Nita reached into the Grandmotherly pocket of her apron and began feeding shells into the Winchester.

KER-POW! The rolling blast of a .30-.30 rifle interrupted their conversation. Pow, pow, pow the Pines echoed the sound back and forth. Dave expected it but he still jumped. The sound came from the house. A moment of silence and KER-POW! The rifle spoke again.

George rolled the window down. "For God's sake don't kill him Nita." He prayed. "Run Revenuer run. Please don't pick up a gun or try to fight back."

KER-POW! This one was a little way down the hill behind the house. Silence, unbearable long silence. KER-POW! This one was even farther down the hill behind the house.

"She's going to run him all the way to the big creek." George said. "Please don't kill him Nita." Silence fell on the moon lit woods. Dave sat and listened. It appeared Nita had run Chester as far as she intended to run him or killed him. Now Dave would have to try and figure out where to pick Chester up. He was a long way from the appointed meeting place. *This is the last hair brained operation I'll participate in,* Dave vowed.

The truck lights swung across the barn and settled on the porch again. Nita stood on the porch, rifle in hand. Little pin points of light floated in her eyes. Her face was black with anger.

"Tell her to lay the rifle on the porch." Dave knew he couldn't bring himself to shoot back if she shot at him.

George leaped out the door. "It's me Mother; put the rifle on the floor." Nita stood thinking.

"Please Mother; put the rifle on the floor."

"Are they going to take you in George?"

"No, lay the rifle on the porch." George walked to the gate.

The long habit of obeying George kicked in and Nita reluctantly laid the rifle gently on the floor.

"Did you hit him Mother?" George was anxious.

"No, the durn Revnoor was sneaking around in our back yard. I just ran him off and I gave him something to think about. Next time I'm shooting right down the middle. Coming here in the night, this is ridiculous."

Dave deftly removed the handcuffs. "Sorry," he mumbled.

"No! Not no but hell no!" George roared. His hands went to his hips. "I'm the one who is sorry. I was so afraid Nita would hurt that guy or that he would hurt her.

"It would be a shame to give a working ranch, livestock and all, to some carpet bagging lawyer in an effort to stay out of prison. There will be no reason for you to return here. You are welcome to come to visit but I'll guarantee you will never find anything here. Besides, I want a piece of your dream."

CHAPTER 11

Lesa finished her evening meal, graded the children's work for the day and was preparing lesson plans for the next day. A soft knock on the back door drew her attention. Opening the door she found Pots, Joe Joe and Joe Jay seated at the picnic table in her backyard. A playful warm breeze shook the leaves lazily above their heads and set the grass rippling beyond the fence. She heard the clank of an iron clad hoof stamping a fly behind the screen of brush beyond the yard. Her heart sank. She wanted to run but her feet betrayed her and her head managed a nod of acknowledgement.

"We've come to have a pow-wow. We're going to

start the still up again." Pots began. "We're all broke and we need money."

"I don't think that is a wise thing to do now. The Feds are hot and heavy right now. They have shut down or caught most of the stills." The expected but much dreaded event was at hand. She could find no way to stop it.

"Yeah Miloy, the sneak punching coward has been busy. He couldn't catch us though. We're going to do it a little different this time. When we were running before we just moved too fast for them. Now we're going to sour our mash at different locations, bring it to a central point, distill it off and send the whiskey out and be gone. We'll be in and out of there so fast the Feds will never find us." Pots began laying out thoughts that had been running around in his mind for some time.

"I don't know about that. They have raided a bunch of stills." Lesa ventured.

"Those guys they caught were fly-by-nighters. They weren't professionals like us. Miloy couldn't catch us before and he won't get us this time. He has done us a favor though. By shutting those other stills down he has caused a shortage of whiskey and we can charge more for what we run. Those boys south of the river are hurting." Pots rubbed his hands together. He could already feel the money in his hands.

"We're going to need more than one still. We'll have to push the whiskey through fast."

"You can't make good whiskey that way." Joe Joe spoke for the first time. Evidently they'd hashed this out before.

"We won't have to. There is such a shortage we can make worse whiskey and sell it for more money. Anyway as soon as we get a batch run off we'll break up the stills and hide the parts at different locations. If the Feds find some of the parts they could never convict us anyway.

"You boys scout around and find us some good big stills. There ought to be some who shut down that would sell their still cheap." Pots was warming to it. "Lesa you may have to let school out a little early sometimes. The whiskey will have to go as soon as it comes off the still. We need to get the whiskey out of the valley very quickly."

"I'm not going to start back. I'm going pass on this one." With a heavy breath Lesa dropped the bomb.

There was silence for awhile and Pots chuckled. "We kind of thought you might say that. We heard about the shindig over to the Stateline Steak House."

"That is none of your business." Lesa turned red.

"Everything is my business. They got Louis with a piddling load. He should have known better. But then so should we. Billy Jack is gone for two years. We've lost a lot of money in this shutdown deal. With Louis and Billy Jack in jail, we have no other dependable way to haul the stuff. We're going to take the car." Pots looked her in the eye.

"No! That is my car. I built it myself." The thought of one of these heavy handed brutes driving the car set her teeth on edge.

Pots grew serious. "You built the car on money you got from us. We're taking the car."

"I built the car with my part of the profit! I did it with my share. None of you put a cent into it!"

"The car is ready to haul. We're going to change the way we haul. None of us can drive like you so we're going to setup ambush cars which will leap frog the loaded car. Some of us should get a good shot at that sneaking Miloy." Pots smiled at the thought.

Lesa turned white. "Ambush?" She mumbled.

"That's right sister. Some of us will shoot Miloy. I want to warn you. If we are caught you will serve time right along with us. You couldn't expect us to keep quiet now could you Missy? That is you'll serve time if you live long enough to do it." Pots enjoyed himself. The Swann brothers looked at the ground. They had counseled against this move but had been overridden by Pots. They didn't like it but they would do their best to carry the plan to a successful conclusion.

"Ambush? How are you going to ambush a Federal Agent?" Lesa was more concerned about Dave than herself. "The place will be crawling with

Federal Agents."

"Aw, they weren't here before that Miloy came home. They might be here a few days after he's gone but they will give up. I've been doing a lot of thinking about this deal you know."

Lesa was terrified. A chill passed over her. Crossing her arms she shivered. She knew she couldn't go to Dave and confess. Tell him the whole story including her part in it. If she didn't he'd be ambushed and killed. What could she do? Her mind searched for a way out. Time was the way to go. Perhaps she could buy time enough to work it out. "Ok I'll run some loads for you. How long do I have to run?"

"That's better! You'll only have to run until we can replace you. Then you can go chase Miloy if that's what you want." Pots lied. "Your first load will be right now."

"Right now?"

"It's loaded in the car. We thought we'd better not give you too much time to think about it." Pots grinned in triumph.

It was Lizzy's hair, makeup and clothes that walked across the road but Lesa's eyes looked through the makeup. The run went without incident. Lesa was drenched with sweat when she returned. How could she have ever thought this was fun and exciting?

What was she going to do? Where was the way out? She was under no illusions about Pots. He wouldn't let her go no matter what he said. That he would try to kill Dave she had no doubts. Like most bully men Pots had contempt for women. He used her superior driving ability but he gave her not one grain of respect for it.

Pots let his contempt over ride his judgment. He didn't watch her like he would have watched a man. What could a dumb woman do anyway?

I could stick that Derringer between Pots shoulder blades and touch off both barrels, she thought. That would solve the whole dilemma concerning herself, Dave and the car. She knew in her heart the only way she could do this was in defense of herself or Dave. Why was she thinking so much about Dave?

He probable had not thought about her since he rushed in early, dropped her, and ran. What did she do to offend him anyway?

"The deliveries started up again last night." The director informed Dave. "We have about all the evidence we need on this end. When you boys catch that still we will arrest the whole bunch."

"Harold is on vacation. Contact him and tell him we need him. We'll go to work on it immediately." Dave's mind began putting things in order. He was sure Pots was involved in the Still. How much surveillance could they put on Pots without him becoming aware of it?

"Are you still there?" The director asked.

"Yeah, just thinking."

"I'll contact Harold and I'll send some of the Academy boys out to assist you."

"We don't need any of the Academy boys here; this situation is too far touchy for anyone without any experience." Dave was sure of this.

"I'll take it under advisement." The director

hung the phone up.

Two days Dave had lain on the ridge top and watched Pots' home place. On the third day Pots appeared leading three horses. He began gathering things up. Dave wondered what kind of parts Pots was putting on the horses. Dave strained the glass reaching across the two and a half miles that separated him from Pots.

Whiskey Still! Dave knew what it was when Pots picked up the worm. Not enough parts to make a whole still. Where was the rest of the still? Were the Swann brothers carrying the rest of the still? Perhaps that was why they had such a hard time catching up to the still. Pots and the Swann brothers ran off one batch of whiskey and moved the still in pieces. Were the pieces going in several directions? It would make convicting them much harder if they were caught with half a still

From his vantage point Dave could see a large amount of the valley. Pots came and went in and out of Dave's view. Dave was in no hurry. He could follow the tracks of three horses.

A flicker of movement in Polecat Canyon, Dave frantically adjusted the telescope. He got it right just in time to see the back of the last horse enter the canyon. Dave laid the telescope aside. Polecat Springs is where the still will be located. There were some minor springs in the canyon but Polecat Springs was the most likely spot.

Dave was tempted to follow Pots but he decided to follow Standard Operating Procedure this time. He called the director.

"I think I know where the still is being erected. Send Harold and Chester to me as soon as possible. We'll raid it in the morning at daylight."

The moon was a great glowing ball above the trees when the trio came over the gap into polecat hollow. They had removed anything that might rattle be shiny or otherwise give their presence away. In the predawn light they moved stealthy down the canyon. There was no fire or light in the basin. They must have finished the run and extinguished the fire and lights. Perhaps the men were taking a nap beside the still. They would wait until daylight before transporting the whiskey.

Skirting the basin the spring was located in, the Revenuers settled down to watch the spring until good light. The night shadows and mist slowly disappeared. There was a beautiful bowl like basin. In the center of the basin a stream of cold crystal clear water boiled out of the ground. It climbed and leaped over the ledge rock that carried it to the surface. The water chuckled, whispered and bubbled merrily over the rocks and miniature water falls. It ran rapidly, impatient to be away on the long trip to the sea.

There was only one thing wrong with this picture. There was no still in the clearing. Dave stood on an outcropping and studied the canyon below. They must have stopped at one of the minor springs below.

Moving rapidly the agents dropped down the canyon. They knew that with each passing minute their chances of catching the still in operation was diminishing.

They came onto horse tracks. The tracks left

the canyon bottom and mounted the hillside. The Agents mounted the hill at all the speed they could muster. They held their council and climbed silently. Each listened carefully. Human voices carried far in the clear mountain air.

Topping out all three of them stood bent over. They were puffing like steam engines and staring at the pile of still burning ashes beside Buckhorn Springs. Frustration seized Dave. Were they not smart enough to bash this still? How could anyone have as much luck as these barn burning bootleggers? He collapsed on the ground and stared out over the valley.

Vera Lee made sure every hair was in place. Her makeup was spotless and her clothes were wrinkle free. It had taken two hours of do and redo to get her into this state. She wasn't satisfied but it was the best she could do.

Descending the stairs she passed through the front room. Her mother sat mending a torn shirt sleeve. When Vera Lee entered the room her mother's eyes widen in surprise then a wise look crossed her face. "I suppose you're going to Harper's store to get the flour we need?"

"Yes mother and I may be awhile. I might meet someone to talk to. It's so lonely here." Vera Lee turned to face her mother. "Where's Dad?"

"He's out behind the barn mending a plow. You better go now so you can get back before supper. Remember, if you're gone too long Dad will come looking for you."

When the sounds of the departing truck ceased mother held the needle up and spoke to it. "That girl is finally coming to her senses." It was amazing how many triumphs, defeats and secrets this needle had shared over the years.

Mr. Harper lay back on the sack of gray shorts and worked in a ledger book. When Vera Lee entered the door he looked at her and his eyes opened in surprise. He looked at the clock and turned to her and smiled. "What can I do for you missy?"

"Mom needs a bag of flour and I wanted to look at the new cloth you got in last week." Vera Lee was radiant and alluring. He felt sorry for Dave.

"Are you in a hurry? I usually fix Dave Miloy a sandwich and he is due here about now." Mr. Harper tested the waters.

"Oh, I'm in no rush at all." Vera Lee moved toward the yard goods

Mr. Harper turned to the task. Nope, his seventy years were not long enough to understand the workings of the female brain.

The door flew open and Dave burst through it. He was in a hurry. He looked haggard and distracted. Mr. Harper tossed the sandwich on the counter and Dave picked it up on his way to the door. "I'm in a hurry. Will you jot it down?" The black car threw dirt and gravel into the air on its way out.

"Yeah," Mr. Harper looked at Vera Lee. She stood with a shocked look and one hand in the air. He knew that many hours of thought and practice went into what ever it was she had no chance to say.

Vera Lee stood stunned. Dave had exploded through the door, grabbed his sandwich and blew out. If he'd seen her he didn't show it. She was no more to him than the pot bellied stove she stood by. He'd always looked before. The night of the Pie Supper he'd looked at her with a hurt longing look on his face. This time there was no reaction at all. She wondered if he saw her standing there. Was it Lesa?

Vera Lee grabbed the flour and dashed out the door. She didn't say a thing or pay for the flour. Mr. Harper could see tears falling on the bag of flour when she went through the door.

"Another seventy years and I wouldn't understand them any better," Mr. Harper muttered to himself and jotted the flour down on the Marley page of the ledger book.

Dave slammed the car into the first few turns. The sun cast sparkling light through the dust and a slow breeze carried it off the roadway. He'd slept very little last night, had a very rigorous hike and a big disappointment at the end of it. He was facing another sleepless night. He was sure the whiskey they run off last night was going to cross the river tonight. He was going to be there to intercept it.

He'd been hungry as a wolf until he walked in

to Harper's Store and saw Vera Lee. No more! He slammed the wheel. No more! He tossed the sandwich out the window. Vera Lee's ability to hurt him died at the Pie Supper. He'd just dried up inside when she turned her back on him in front of all the citizens of the valley. He'd decided she was never going to get that chance again. The citizens of this valley? Most still shunned him because he was a Revenue Agent. All right he would show them what a Revenue Agent was. He thought of Lesa and the light that came into her eyes when fast cars were mentioned.

Tonight he was going to intercept that black Ford. There were several bridges available to the Ford. Anyone who could drive like that driver wasn't afraid of bad roads so he was going to gamble on the roughest crossing. He was going to have help. The Agency sent cars and the Highway Patrol was alerted.

CHAPTER 12

The Agency installed two way radios in all the cars but Dave had no faith in the unreliable radios. The cars had to be rubbing bumpers to communicate with each other. The man who caught the Ford wasn't going to have time to play with a radio. Driving would take all his concentration.

Calm down and clear your mind he warned himself. You cannot run if you are not relaxed. A driver must have no fear, be relaxed and boil his entire being down to extracting the extreme capabilities of the automobile he drove. If a driver was touched by fear or tightened up in the violent maneuvers he was dead. He could get no sleep but he'd get some rest while on stake out.

It might have been Lizzy's shell but it was Lesa who wheeled the Ford onto the roadway. She had stalled longer than usual. The sun set and darkness was rising from the ground. There would be no moon until near daylight. She preferred to run on a dark night. It made it harder for the chase driver to see through the dust of a dirt road. If you could find a hole to duck into without your lights on no moonbeam reflection would give you away. She tested the switches that turned her tail and brake lights off. She was careful not to bump the one that folded her tag down so it could not be read.

The Ford ran like perfection itself. It was light in her hands. God, she loved this car! She'd put the essence of her life in it. It returned her love with a mighty roar when she touched the accelerator petal. Every part of the car had been selected and installed after much thought and loving care. There was no way Pots was going get his grubby hands on this car. She realized Pots didn't care about the car. Oh, he'd take it from her just to be the man in charge. He rightly figured she couldn't very well call on the law to retrieve a car set up to haul bootleg booze.

Pots forced her to drive one more trip. After this run she was going to go to Dave and confess all her evil deeds. Let the chips fall where they may. She wasn't going to live in mortal fear of Pots ambushing Dave. This was her and the car's last run.

Lesa walked the floor every night after Vera Lee's visit. The first question, was she breaking up something she ought not to interfere in? As a woman she knew Dave was interested in her. She knew it before he did. She decided Vera Lee and Dave broke up when he started to college five years ago. Dave wrote a letter or two and got no response. After that there was nothing. Now for the biggie, was Dave still in love with Vera Lee? She doubted it. Her heart made her doubt it. She remembered the look on his face at the Pie Supper. Had Vera Lee turned love into hate?

Now for herself. Was she in love with Dave? Yes.

Was Dave falling in love with her? She believed it was happening. Would she marry him? In a minute! All this stuff was a moot point though. She could feel the scorn Dave would heap on her when he came to know who was driving the black Ford.

If she confessed she would most likely get four years in a Federal Prison. Pots and the Swann brothers would share her fate. Lesa grinned. She bet Pots never thought about it in this light when he threatened her with prison. Well if she decided to go she'd take Mr. Pots right along with her. What would it do to his bullying attitude if a mere woman took four years of his life?

Dave would still be alive to makeup with Vera Lee or do what he wanted. At least he would still be alive. She vowed she would not be taken alive on this run. She was going to explain this mess to Dave on her terms or not at all.

The Engine Puttered along at the speed limit. It only took a small portion of the available horsepower to maintain speed limit. She decided to cross the river on the Coalville road. It was still dirt and

BATTLE OF WHISKEY VALLEY

relatively rough. It would be the road the Revenuers patrolled the least. Once she got beyond the
river there was a bewildering maze of roads. They
couldn't watch them all.

She kept telling herself to relax. Driving at high
speeds was an art. The driver has to reduce his very
being to the mechanics of handling the car. There
can be no fear or hesitation. The thought of a wreck
must never enter her mind. She must be acutely
aware of every nuance of the car. Feel when she
should let go of the brake and pick up the accelerator. How much accelerator was needed, how much
balance between the front wheels and the spinning
back wheels. She must control the skid with the accelerator. Increasing and decreasing the power. She
must become a smoothly functioning part of the
machine.

She had to be very aware of and adept at quickly reading the road ahead of her. How sharp the
curve, what is the road surface, crowned inside or
outside the curve? What did the road surface con-
sist of? Was it dirt, gravel, sand or clay? So many

variables and such a short time to assimilate them when you're barreling into corners you can't see until your headlights hit them. You cannot be tight. You must sit back and become an integral part of the car.

Lesa ran these things through her head. High speed driving was like shooting. You needed to do it in order to stay sharp. She'd been off for some time.

Popping over the hill she slowed. This was one of the most likely trouble spots. When her lights popped over the hill they made a sweeping motion as the front wheels began the descent. There was the briefest flash of chrome beyond the bridge. There was a car on the other side of the river. Slowing even more she searched for the car on this side. There would be one to plug each end of the bridge when she started across. Not tonight suckers, she thought. She failed to locate the car on this side of the bridge. She better not get in close enough to have a car on either side of her.

Lesa flipped the switches off to her tail and brake lights. She folded the license plate down.

Touching the brake she threw car into a spinning rock throwing half donut. Easing the accelerator when the rear end came in line behind the front end, the rear wheels took hold and lined the front with the road in the opposite direction to what she had been traveling. She then punched it hard. She fought to keep it from fishtailing. She needed all the acceleration she could get. As soon as she could look back she saw the lights come onto the road behind her. Another vehicle had been waiting to trap her on the bridge.

Dave agreed to help set the trap. It would work on most drivers but he would have been severely disappointed if the Ford had fallen into it. He had a lot of respect for this driver's ability. He knew he was in for a run.

Lesa did a bad job on the first corner. She managed to stay upright and go. The black car gained on her. She was panicking. Please God take me home before he catches me. She did the same on the next corner. Dave was disappointed, he wanted the regular driver and he knew this wasn't the driver he chased at Frogville. This driver didn't posses the skill and nerve of the one he chased into Granny Whooten's road block He was going to catch this car shortly. Disappointment settled on his shoulders.

Lesa sat back and held the accelerator down. She was blasting down a straight run. Reaching to a switch on the dash she flipped it. The quiet night was instantly blown apart by the roar of the big engine as the solenoids opened the Lakes plugs behind each front wheel. Blue flames leaped out to light the road on either side of the car. The look in Lesa's eyes changed. Her touch on the steering wheel and accelerator changed as Lizzy took over. She looked in the mirror and smiled. "Come on big boy!" She yelled. "Let's see what you're made of."

Another five miles flashed by. Dave was puzzled. Why the two bad corners to begin with? The rest had been handled with the rarely seen precision he expected at the start. What kind of trick was this driver setting up? There was a voice on his radio but he tuned it out. He knew it was over if he slowed enough to talk on the radio. He must keep his entire focus on the handling of the car.

Lizzy ripped tons of dust into the air. How could the black car hang on when she was sure his vision was severely impaired? He couldn't be keying on her tail or brake lights. She had none. Where can I dump him? There is bound to be some place I have the advantage. Where can I go that I can drive through faster than he can? There has to be a place!

The main highway was coming up. Easing the petal she sent flashes of red flame and a machine gun staccato of roaring back raps into the night. She turned onto the hardtop road amid the thunder of the engine and squall of rubber. The torquey thunder changed to a high pitched snarl as the engine picked up RPM.

Dave held his position. He wasn't gaining but he wasn't loosing any ground either. This was going to be a game of luck. One of them was bound to goof sooner or later. It had to happen. He glanced at his speedometer. It read a steady speed of well over one hundred miles per hour. He didn't know where they were going but it wasn't going to take long to get there.

Lizzy tossed the Ford onto the Frogvllie road. She was still trying to figure where and how she was going to lose him

Dave grinned. The old Granny Whooton trick again. *I have him,* Dave thought. There is a patrol car at Granny Whooton's house and a patrolman sitting on the running board of that old truck. Just past Granny's there is a barricade across the road a tank couldn't run through.

Dave backed off a little. He let the little breeze that was blowing move the dust to one side or the other. There was no use pushing hard when they had the goose in the bag. He wanted to see this driver's face. He…? Suddenly the road ahead of him was free of dust! The Ford had turned up the side road back there and he was busy being so sure of himself he overshot the turn. Slamming the brakes on, he threw it into reverse and whipped back to the turn. He set the black car upon the road after the Ford. He'd made the mistake. He pounded the wheel in frustration. *Day dreaming,* he berated himself. He counted his ducks at the wrong time! He sure didn't like the hatching he had gotten.

Lizzy barreled on through the night. She didn't know what had happened at the corner but she hoped Dave had just over shot the turn. She couldn't help but worry about him. She was tempted to duck into one of the side roads to check on him. She continued to push it to the limit until she hit the highway again. Turning left she blistered the pavement.

Dave came onto the highway. It wasn't hard to see which way the Ford went but he knew it was the last sign he would see. He went up the road at a good clip but it was nothing like the blistering speeds they came into the area with. He was thoroughly disgusted. Two days without sleep. A rigorous hike and a long car chase. He had nothing. Absolutely nothing. *How could I miss that turn? Am I cut out be an Agent?* Dave wasn't having much luck. *Now I have to face the Director and tell him I have nothing.* He was tired. Bone tired. Suddenly he knew fatigue was the reason he missed the turn. When the brain gets too tired it focuses on each item for too long a time.

Lizzy sat on the county loop and watched the black car cruise by. She thought about it for awhile. Firing the Ford up she flipped the switch to close the Lakes Plugs. The engine sound died from a roar to a rumble. She slipped out onto the highway and ran for the Coalville Road. The Feds never would think of her coming back to a crossing where they had set a trap for her.

The Ford popped over the hill above the bridge at the maximum speed Lizzy could maintain control. It was do or die. If someone drove a car into the roadway in front of her, they would be broken from that habit. She was too tired to care much either way. Two switches on the dash brought the headlights on and opened the Lakes Plugs. The blast of the open pipes and blazes of blue fire shattered the stillness of the night.

Trailing fire and smoke out both sides the Ford flashed across the bridge. Lizzy got a fleeting glance of the two startled Highway Patrolmen standing beside a small fire with coffee cups in their hands and their jaw hanging.

They would try to chase her but they had just as well finish their coffee before they start. She was almost there. The last run.

The run had taken up most of Friday night. Sunday morning Lesa backed the Ford into the small barn. She ran her hands lovingly over the hood. Petting it like an animated thing. She laid her head on the top and tears ran across the windshield. Tripping on some loose hay Lesa kicked it into a small pile and tossed a match into it. She watched until the heat began blistering the paint, then she said goodbye to Lizzy and the Ford. She turned to the door. The last run.

Dave did not want to make this report to the Director. "It seems like they've got the luck of the devil. Every break has gone their way." Dave told the director.

"Do I need to send you some more help?" The director was trying to be helpful. "We've pretty much got the evidence we need on this end. We're waiting for you boys to tie up that end."

"We'll get lucky, sooner or later. We've been

tightening the noose, so to speak."

"You boys have made significant headway. There is no longer a river of whiskey flowing out of the valley. If you can shut this ring down I'd say this campaign will be a success." The director was being expansive. "It will take years to shut the bootlegging down completely but you guys have taken the governor off my back for now. We'll transfer you to another district as soon as you finish here."

Dave thought about the transfer. He'd decided he wanted to stay in the valley but when he thought of Vera Lee he was not so sure. Perhaps he should move on. This was not the time to discuss it. "We're bound to get a break on the case soon. The laws of averages say it's our turn."

The day after the fire the black car rumbled to a stop. Dave looked across the small pasture at the burned out hulk of the Ford. Small tendrils of smoke still rose here and there. The sluggish breeze carried the nauseating smell of the disaster across the road. The somber clouds cast a desolate pall over the beauty the Ford used to be. Dave had a soft spot for excellent machinery. The sight of the Ford's misery touched chords of lonesomeness in him. In his minds eye he could see the Ford vibrant and alive with the engine thundering, wheels spinning, broad sliding the corner at Frogville. Dave raised a hand in salute to the Ford. He didn't like for it to end thus way. He would never get a chance to outrun the Ford now. There would always be a doubt as to whether he and the black car were good enough or not. Even the black car's rumbling exhaust seemed quieter in respect for the burned out hulk. Dave steered the black car into the school driveway.

Lesa leaned against the door jam. Her heart stood still for a moment. The day of reckoning was at hand. Her knees were weak and shaking, another fork in the road of life. Which fork would she take? Which fork would be open to her? She was terrified and didn't know what to do about it.

"Looks like things got warm over across the road." Dave eased the car door shut.Lesa nodded.

"That car looks familiar to me." Dave stepped

past Lesa into the room.

"Dave I need to talk to you." Lesa began

"Yep, that was a whiskey running car." Dave interrupted.

"Dave I ..." Lesa began again.

"I ran that car all over those dirt roads down by Frogville one night. I managed to punch through the dust on the second turn and get a quick look at the driver." Dave was looking across the road at the Ford but he was watching Lesa out of the corner of his eye.

Her heart sank. He knew who was driving the Ford and had come to arrest her. She clung to the door jam tightly. Her throat constricted. One hand flew to her throat.

"That driver sure was ugly. Eyes drew down to a slit, nose protruding, thin lips turned down at the corners."

Anger flashed through Lesa. Her mouth flew open and an angry retort was hanging on her lips.

Dave continued before Lesa could retort. "One thing I'll never forget was his red hair and red mustache. Have you seen anyone like that around the old barn over there?"

Lesa's knee gave way on her. "I ... I". Clinging to the jam she wilted. Dave caught her before she fell to the floor. She looked up at the amused grin and the twinkle in his eyes. "You bastard!" She screamed ripping herself from his arms. "You put me through the hellish torment of trying to find a way to tell you something you already knew?"

The amused grin and the twinkle increased, "That isn't half as bad as cheating."

"Cheating?" Lesa was puzzled. "You don't think Grandma Whooten was a fair thing to do to anybody, do you?"

"You deserved it!" Lesa got hold of her temper rapidly. "Picking on a poor defenseless redheaded man you couldn't even catch."

"I'm going over to look at the car and see if there any sign of ownership left around it. Want to come?"

Lesa sobered instantly. "No! I've been there. It is not a good place for me."

Dave went over the area. Note pad in hand he prepared to report on his findings. The residual alcohol in the tanks had exploded and left gaping holes. The interior was totally gone. The dash and instrument gauges were melted. He grinned when he saw the large tachometer case on the steering column. The works had melted and dripped into fire. He could imagine Lizzy's quick glances at the instrument when slamming from corner to corner. The ball on the shift stick had melted and ran down the stick to the four speed La Salle transmission. The tires had burned off so the bottom of the car almost touched the ground. He grinned. Someone knew exactly how much to lower the body. He could see nothing underneath the car. He noted the wide wheels.

The hood was pinned down so it couldn't pop loose and come up under the stress of violent maneuvers. Finding a stray limb on the ground he raised the hood and placed the limb under it. The springs designed to hold the hood up had lost their temper and bent in the inferno.

He looked at the engine. Whoa! He didn't know what he'd been expecting but this wasn't it. It looked like a General Motors type engine but he'd never seen one like it.

He looked at it long and carefully from both sides. On closer observation it was obviously a General Motors product. The heat burned all wiring, melted the soldier out of the generator, reduced the carburetors to piles of molten metal in the valley pan, burned the distributor cap and wiring, melted the engine number, and stripped all the paint off the engine. Dave backed away from the foul smelling fumes still rising from the mess.

After a breath of fresh air he returned to the car. He examined the suspension. It was no wonder he couldn't get inside this car on the corners. The car had been lowered and the suspension stiffened. There were struts and sway bars the like of which he'd never seen before. A long set of traction bars secured the rear end.

It was clear this car wasn't built by a backyard mechanic. It had been built by someone who had a very good knowledge of the world of high speed cars, one of the mechanics from the racetracks? He'd look farther into this.

Lesa sat at the picnic table and watched him poke and prod on the body of her baby. Tears ran freely down her cheeks. She hated him! He didn't have to stay this long with the body. He could ... Then she realized what kind of turmoil she would be going through if he hadn't talked to her first. Then she hated him again. She'd spent sleepless nights and foodless days trying to figure the best time and place to tell him about the Ford and her complicity in the bootlegging ring. He'd known all along! She didn't have to make the last few runs Pots forced her into. She hated him more. He chased her so hard! He'd caused her to burn the Ford. She hated him all over again.

He was coming past his car. He is coming back to her and he has a set of handcuffs in his hand. She could see the sun gleaming off the shiny metal. He was playing a cat and mouse game with her! Why? Was he hoping she would implicate Pots and the

Swann brothers? Well he'd better think again. This would never happen now. She laid her head on her arms.

"Try this one on." The metal clanked on the table beside her head. Resigned to her fate she raised her head and reached for the metal. It was the chrome ring from around a taillight of the Ford!

"How do you figure the whole car burned except that taillight ring? Must have blown off when the back whiskey tank blew." He wiped some of the tears from her face. "Since it burned so close to the school I thought you might want to keep that as a souvenir. All the evidence says it was arson. Someone torched that car." He was silent for a moment. "It's a good thing for that redheaded fellow the Ford burned. If it hadn't burned I'd have to turn it in to the laboratory so they could check for prints and other identifying marks.

"I've already talked to my Director and the School Board. I'm going to have Milton Love bring his dozer and bury the whole mess except for the engine. I've never seen one like it and it is possible the block wasn't ruined by the fire. If I catch up to the redheaded jasper perhaps he can tell me where the dress up parts came from. Can I store the engine in the storage shed here?" Dave had the amused twinkle in his eyes. "He did a superb job of building that car. It wasn't just a car. It was a work of love. I'm sorry it had to burn. But believe me that is by far best way."

CHAPTER 13

P ots, Joe Joe and Joe Jay sat on one side of the picnic table in Lesa's backyard.

Lesa sat on the other. No one was relaxed. The air crackled with tension. Even the wind held its breath so the oak trees could be still and listen.

"We've talked it over and we'll help you build another car. We'll pay half the cost and help you work on it." Pots was being generous.

"No, no more cars, no more runs." Lesa placed her elbow on the table and leaned forward with her chin resting on her hand. She looked Pots in the eye. Pots saw the hardness coming into her eyes and suddenly the table seemed narrower.

"Things can happen you know." Pots warned. "Nobody quits on us!"

With a sharp intake of breath Lesa sat up as if Pots had slapped her. The cold gray eyes grew frostier. They bored into his. Pots shivered at the message he saw there. Never had Pots looked into a pair of eyes that shook him like these were. He managed to tear his gaze loose and drop it to the tabletop.

"If you try any of your barn burning back stabbing tricks or mess with me in anyway an undertaker will be wiping you. You were going to take the Ford from me. You can have it now! You find yourself a car and one of you make a run. You won't be making many. Miloy and his boys have a good idea where the whiskey is going now. "You'll be visiting with Louis and Billy Jack before you make the third run. Exactly which part of no do you not understand?" Lesa's jaw snapped shut and she gazed at Pots like a Cobra watching a Mongoose.

"Miloy could be wiped out! We know how to handle Miloy!" Pots jumped from the table and tried to gauge the effect of the threat on Lesa.

Lesa settled on the bench again. I got her Pots thought. After a few seconds Lesa spoke in a low conversational voice. "You know Pots, one of the nice things about teaching school is that you have to be able to read and write. I've written this whole mess up, all of it, mine, yours and these boys. I gave it to a lawyer. It is notarized in the form of an affidavit and it can be used in a court of law. If anything happens to me or Miloy the District Attorney gets the file." She smiled at him. "I'll honor the code of the hills. No one rats on anyone, even an enemy; to the IRS but if you want to get tough I'll see all of you in the Electric Chair! Besides, the last time you tried to handle Miloy it didn't work out too well." Lesa finished sarcastically.

Lesa looked at Joe Joe and Joe Jay. "Are you boys going to let him pull you down with him?"

Pots snorted like a startled deer, turned purple, and strode toward his horse. "The sneaking coward hit me while I wasn't looking!" He'd told this lie so often he'd come to believe it.

Dave watched Pots load the horses. He'd figured

out what parts of the still each of the three carried. They shut the operation of the still down when the Ford burned. It was the last of their transportation vehicles.

Pots was getting desperate. Without the still his income came to a sudden halt. The Swann brothers were faced with the same problem. Pots and the Swanns put everything, including their time, into the still. They had abandoned other means of support. There was no way Pots was going back to forty acres and a mule. No sir! There was too much hard work low pay associated with farming.

They'd approached Lesa again but no amount of threat or bribe could budge her. She was through. She informed them of this fact and handed a block buster threat right back to them. If they pulled any their barn burning or other little tricks on her she would hit back hard. Pots could see no way to push her farther.

"We have to do something." Pots told the Swann brothers when they left Lesa's. "Almost all the stills have shut down or been caught. Even the local

Bootleggers are having trouble getting enough whiskey to sell. We can set up and sell some whiskey to them. We'll have to sell it quite a bit cheaper than we were. Maybe that will keep us going until the Feds get tired of chasing us and we can send our whiskey across the river again. I've never seen a Fed like Miloy. He won't quit."

"How is that mash coming along? Is it anywhere near ready?

"The mash is ready to run." Joe Jay seldom broke the silence.

"Alright let's run her. You meet me at Squaw Springs we'll set up just before dark tonight and run her off in early in the morning."

Dave lay on his back and watched the big white puff ball clouds march across the silent sky. A fox squirrel stopped on an overhead limb and began scolding him for disturbing the peace and tranquility of the forest. Each time it barked its tail jerked. He was chewing Dave out for lying under the best oak in the forest. Finding a good throwing rock Dave bounced it off the limb at the squirrel's feet.

The squirrel decided he'd said enough on this matter and leaped behind the tree body.

Surveillance duty had to be the worst, the most boring duty on earth, Dave decided. As much as he liked to watch the forest folk it grew irksome after a certain amount of time. His eyes swept Pots' place again. There was movement!

Dave carefully trained the big telescope on Pots and cleared it up. The setting sun was on his left and the air was clear. He didn't have to worry about the sun reflecting off the telescope and warning Pots. He could crank the telescope up until he could see the scar on Pots' face. Dave watched as Pots circled up the valley on little used trails. He grew more interested when Pots turned up the trail which climbed a long point off Big John Mountain.

He became even more interested when Pots turned west off the traveled trail. Riding around the mountain Pots turned up the first big hollow. Dave ran the scope up the hollow in front of Pots.

Whoa! There were horses there. Impatiently he wrestled the scope back to the horses. The field of view was so small on the big scope it took a minute to find the horses again. It was the Swann Brothers and they were setting up a still! He leaped to his feet. This was the break they had been waiting for.

The hollow was open to the valley. They were setting up the still. They wouldn't run tonight. There was too much chance of the fire being located in the dark. They would run it tomorrow morning. He mentally calculated the hours. There should be time to bring Chester and Harold in and be at the still by the time it broke daylight. He didn't stay until Pots climbed to the still. Loping off the mountain he piled into the agency pickup and ran for the telephone.

The Director was slow to answer. Please let someone be there Dave breathed into the phone.

"Hello." The director's voice sounded sweet on this call.

"I've found the still. I need Chester and Harold to meet me at midnight. I'll be on the head of the old Taylor Haul road." Dave was excited.

"It will be inconvenient. I can have them meet

you at noon.

"Noon? Man, noon will be too late. I'm telling you I've found THE still. They will be gone if we wait until noon to start in."

"I can send some of the Academy boys to help you. They could get there by midnight." The Director was set on the Academy boys.

"No! I'd rather do it alone than wet nurse greenhorns." Dave was just as adamant, "There will be no Academy boys. "It's going to make me late to my dinner but I'll get Chester and Harold to you." The Director complained.

"I won't be late for dinner because I won't have one. I'll be locating the safest and easiest way to get that still. We want the still and its operators. And will you call the motor pool and tell them I need a station wagon to bring these guys in with." Dave was thinking ahead. "I'll need the one with the most ground clearance."

Dave dashed to his rooms and rapidly donned camouflaged clothing. He stood in front of the mirror and carefully blacked his face. He didn't think

Pots would leave a guard. If there was one it was imperative he see the guard before the guard saw him. If the half Indian Swanns were on guard duty he doubted his ability to slip past them. He planned to go to the still and pick out hiding places while it was still dark. He wanted to be hid in sight of the still when Pots and crew came to work it. He was going to enjoy handcuffing Pots. This was a pleasure he was thoroughly looking forward to.

Dave reconnoitered the still and then ran down to the head of the old Taylor Haul road. He saw two pickups. Why did Harold and Chester come in two pickups? No matter this was far enough away it shouldn't warn Pots or the Swanns.

Harold and Chester were there, camouflaged and blacked out. Two men stood between them with white shirts on.

"What's this?" Dave demanded from Harold with a wave of his hand toward the men in suits.

"We're from the Academy." The taller thin one answered for Harold.

"Good, you get back in the truck and take a nap

we'll holler for you when we need you." Dave was livid.

"The director told us you would most likely say that." The husky surly one rasped. "He also gave us a direct order to assist you in the breaking up this still. You can't countermand the Directors orders. Besides, I hear you haven't been doing much of a job catching this still."

Dave turned and walked down the road. Harold followed.

"This will never do!" Dave threw his cap down. "I didn't find that still Harold lets pack'em up and all go home!"

Harold let Dave stew a bit then, "Aw, it won't be too bad Dave we'll ride herd on them. I'll take one and Chester can take the other. We'll baby sit them and you won't have to worry about them."

Dave stewed. They'd worked long and hard for this day. He was so excited. This seemed to be the perfect setup. "You've been around long enough to get a feel for Pots and the Swann brothers. If it's done right there will be no shooting. If it's done wrong they will shoot at a battalion of Marines."

Dave strode back to the pickups and stuck his finger in the surly ones face. "You will go with Harold. You WILL do exactly as he tells you to do."

The agent's surly face turned red. "I'll do …"

"You WILL do EXACTLY what you are told to do!" Dave cut him short.

"The Director …"

"If you have anything to say to, for or about the Director you get in that pickup and go tell him right now!" Dave spoke sternly.

The surly agent started to say something and looked into Dave's eyes. His jaw snapped shut and he turned away.

They strung out in single file. Dave led the group. The tall thin agent came next behind him with Chester looking over his shoulder. The surly one tromped along staring at the ground. He's not watching anything. *If we left him here by himself he couldn't find his way back to the pickup* Harold thought. Each carried a different type of firearm. In a situation like this it could be quick, up close and dirty or a long range slugfest. Each also carried his service revolver.

Dave figured the most likely direction the moonshiners would come from. Then he found a large rock on the opposite side of the still. He motioned for the Academy boys to lay on the ground behind the rock.

Dave and Chester each found a large Yellow Pine to hide behind. Harold chose a big Red Oak. Past experience taught them they could move around the tree and stay hidden regardless of which direction the moonshiners approached the still. Each settled into their thoughts and the long wait began.

Dave watched the dawn spilling color across the eastern sky. A buzzing sound rose from the forest. It took Dave a moment to locate the source. The surly Academy boy was asleep and snoring!

Dave selected a nice size stone and bounced it off the agent's leg. The man let out a startled snort and glared at Dave. Dave's eyes held daggers and his thumb was turned down. Silence reigned again.

The silence was the silence of the forest. In the

forest there is very seldom complete silence. Breezes played whispering tag among the trees. Birds flitted from tree to tree. A squirrel barked over Harold's head and there was a rustle of leaves when it leaped into the next tree. With a piercing cry a Red Tail hawk stooped hard on the squirrel. Crickets chirped around Dave's feet. Cicada added their high pitched buzz to the mix. A rustling in the leaves drew Dave's attention to a huge Diamond Backed Rattler coming his way. The snake's six feet six made it longer than Dave is tall. It was as big around as a stovepipe.

The Triangular head spanned more area than a man's hand. Black streaks ran from the nostrils to the eyes. A surprisingly thin and supple neck attached the massive head to the immense body. The dark diamonds stood in stark contrast to the lighter scales surrounding it. This snake shed it s skin recently, leaving the scales bright and shiny. A long string of rattles stood at half mast on the stubby tail.

The snake passed within ten feet of Dave. It was oblivious to his existence. Dave motioned with his hand to draw the rookie's attention. He motioned for them to stay down and pointed to the snake crossing a bare spot twenty feet from them. Both men started to leap to their feet. Dave pointed a demanding finger at the ground.

At their movement the snake whipped into an S curve with its head suspended eighteen inches above the ground. The rattles buzzed an angry warning. Their eyes grew panicky. Every time they turned to Dave he was pointing stay down.

No threat appeared so the Rattler rustled its way to the spring. Backing under the bark of a fallen Pine it was ready for the next thirsty rodent coming to water.

It began as a low hum and slowly evolved into human voices. Human voices carry far in the silence of the woods. Soon Dave could hear the click of steel shod hoofs on rock. Tilting his head he could make out the rumbling voice of Pots. The Revenue Agents adjusted their position behind the trees to match the direction the voices were approaching from.

Pots materialized through the forest. Joe Joe was right behind him. They were carrying on the razz about their names. Dave breathed a sigh of relief when Joe Jay rode into sight. Pots and Joe Joe dismounted and tied their horses. They waited impatiently for Joe Jay. The delay put unbearable tension on the Agents.

"You're going to have to trade that horse for something that can walk." Pots shouted derisively Joe Jay. All three men walked toward the still.

"INTERNAL REVENUE SERVICE!" The thick surly Agent popped over the top of the rock with his badge in one hand and a service revolver in the other. He'd forgotten about the rifle at his feet. These fellows were supposed to faint at the sight of a badge. Pots rifle leaped to his shoulder.

"Hold it Pots!!" Dave roared just as Pots sights settled on the pocket of the white shirt. The sound of his name stopped Pots more than anything else. He looked into the business end of the shotgun Dave centered on him and dropped the rifle. Joe Joe ran the opposite direction. Harold's foot shot out from behind the red oak and sent him head over teakettle. Harold had the rifle barrel stuck in his chest before Joe Joe recovered. Joe Jay spun around a couple of times trying to make up his mind, fight or run. If he fired on Dave or Harold they would kill Pots and or Joe Joe for sure. When he turned to run he was looking into Chester's eyes over the barrel of a Thompson submachine gun. Reluctantly Joe Jay lay his rifle down.

"I did it. I did it! This bust is mine! I confronted them first." The surly agent was beside himself.

Dave's shotgun swung up in a smooth arc. "NO! Dave!

NO!" Harold screamed. The surly agent stood bewildered. After a few moments pause Dave clicked the safety on and handcuffed Pots while Harold took care of the other two.

"This is my bust! You guys can't claim it." The surly Agent buzzed up importantly.

Dave started the blow from the ground. It caught the celebrating Agent solidly. The blow sounded like an ax handle hitting a side of beef. The agent fell into the duff; lay still for a moment then rose to a dazed sitting position. After a moment his eyes cleared and they were ugly. His hand moved toward his service revolver and hesitated when he realized Dave was holding a load of Double Ought Buck shot centered on his chest and his finger was on the trigger.

"Go ahead," Dave encouraged him.

The agent climbed to his feet and glared at Dave.

"You damned right this is your bust and you are going to hear about it for a long time if the Director don't fire you outright, which is what I'm going to recommend. You would be dead if we hadn't bailed you out. Pots had you dead to rights. You ask him if he would have shot you or not. You dumb bastard you wasted the months of time and effort we've put into this case up to now." Dave was furious.

"Wasted? How?" The surly Agent asked.

"You gave these boys a get out of jail free card!" Dave snorted.

"We caught them …'

"No we didn't catch them! You pulled a dumb stunt. You yelled too quickly. They touched no part of the still. We didn't catch them in the act of making

Moonshine. We caught them walking through the woods. We can't convict them now." Dave looked at a smiling Pots. "We're going to take them in and they'll spend some time in jail and spend a lot of money on a lawyer but they will be back after the trial."

"I should have listened to you and just flat refused to bring them along," Harold apologized.

It was a silent group that marched out to the vehicles. "Keep them here. I'll get the station wagon."

When Dave returned they loaded the prisoners.

Dave watched the surly Agent bend to spit blood from the split lip. When the agent returned to full height Dave withdrew an ax from the pickup bed. The agent looked at the ax and involuntarily stepped back trying to make up his mind. Fight or flight?

"Since this is your bust you have a lot of work to do to finish it off." Dave reversed the ax handle and held it out to the agent.

"What do we do?"

"Whatever you heart desires." Dave handed an

ax to the taller agent. "Don't forget you have some animals tied out there that have to be handled properly."

"What do you mean? What are you going to do? I've never touched a horse in my life!"

"Remember class 301 at the Academy, the class on how to destroy and properly secure a raided still? Just follow the book. We're going to take the prisoners in."

With Pots and the Swann Brothers duly booked into the County Jail, the agents were on the way back to the valley when a car flashed by them. "Pots and the Swanns." Chester breathed.

"Why do we bother?" Harold slapped the seat. "How did they get out so fast?"

"Most of the bigger moonshiners put bail money aside and they have a bail bondsman on twenty four hour alert. It's something we've seen over and over again. But, this time it seems awful quick." Dave held a steady pace and watched the other car disappear into the distance.

"Dave, you will have to really watch your back now. The look in Pots eyes when we handcuffed him made me shudder. He's going to be madder now than he was the night you beat him down. That Pots is bad news." Chester warned.

"I hope those Academy boys have done their work and gone home. It's like them to be waiting at Pots' house to find out what to do with the horses. They better learn all the bootleggers and still operators are not going to melt at the sight of a badge." Dave decided they had best go check on the academy boy's work.

When Dave, Chester and Harold reached the top end of Taylor Haul Road, both pickups were still parked there. Both trucks were parked in the same position they were in when the group of agents departed for town with the prisoners.

"I don't believe they've been here." Harold shut the truck door.

The three men stared at each other with the same thought in mind. "Pots and the Swanns are back." Chester finally put it into words.

"Let's see if they made it to the still." Dave started walking rapidly.

The still hadn't been touched. It was ready to run. The horses were still tied in the same spot. By the amount of droppings it was clear they hadn't been moved. "What do we do now?" Harold scratched his head.

"I shouldn't have left them here alone." Dave looked at the setting sun. "It will be dark before long. One thing for sure no one from the valley will hunt a lost IRS agent. Chester you take one of the trucks and contact the Director. Tell him to call the Governor and put the National Guard on standby.

"They are almost ready to graduate. You would think they could handle a job that simple, most especially since they'd already seen the trail from both directions." Harold dreaded Dave's next words.

"Harold you go uphill and cover that end as much as you can. I'll go downhill. Take your time, cover the ground and remember Pots and the Swanns are loose. I wouldn't expect them to come to what they believe is a smashed still but be careful. They aren't in a good mood right now. I'll meet you back here in three hours." Dave retrieved a rifle from his station wagon and trudged reluctantly downhill.

It was almost a perfect evening. The temperature was just right and a little breeze rustled through the trees. The Sun began to push fiery fingers across the sky.

Pots was in a churlish mood. He'd sent the Swanns home without a goodbye. He didn't know why he was climbing the mountain. It would just make him madder to see the wrecked still. His horses had not come home and he decided to see if those Revenoors were sorry enough to leave the horses tied without food or water. The Agents must have stolen the horses. They'd at least steal the saddles.

Pots fumed along until he looked up and saw a rabbit running his direction. This wasn't right the rabbit should have been running away. Pots stopped dead still. The only thing that moved was his eyes. He saw a flash of movement and a flash of color. It was Dave Miloy! What was he doing here at this time of day? Pots didn't care. It looked like something was going to go his way after all.

Dave crunched along on top of a small ridge across a little ravine. Pots let Dave pass his position and he ducked behind the trees and ran down ahead of Dave. He found a rock with a bush growing over it. The rifle barrel slid through the screening brush and settled on the rock. Pots settled down to think. He couldn't visualize any situation that would bring Dave back here today.

Dave ambled into sight. He was taking his time and looking for sign of the Academy boys.

Pots eased the rifle inline with Dave and holding the trigger so Dave would have no chance to hear the clicks his thumb slowly drew the hammer back and began settling the buckhorn sights on Dave's chest. His finger slowly took up the slack. Dave decided to go above the Winter Huckleberry thicket. He abruptly turned and stepped behind the brush.

What the ...?? Couldn't anything go right for Pots today? He pulled back behind the ridge and ran. Had Dave seen him? He didn't think so but one thing he'd learned. Never underestimate Dave Miloy. He decided to ease on up and look at the still. Sometimes the Agents got lazy and didn't destroyed all the parts of a working still.

Dave finished his three hour circle and walked back through the velvet smooth night. He thought of the big rattler of the morning and wondered where it was now. Pushing through the last of the brush he stepped into the clearing at the top of the haul road. The truck was gone! The Academy boy's truck was missing. He turned slowly to be sure he was where he thought he was. There was no way around it. The truck was gone. His station wagon was sitting there all alone. A rustle in the brush and a shocked Harold stood at the edge of the clearing.

CHAPTER 14

"Well at least both of them got back ok. I see tracks on both sides of the truck." Harold ventured into the stillness, "Unless Pots got them and the truck."

"I'm going to check the still." Dave walked very fast until he was close and then slowed down. The still was gone. The horses were gone. Even the sour mash was gone. Everything was gone! Dave's crew didn't even get a pile of ashes this time!

A set of headlights wound up the dusty trail and stopped. Chester stepped out "The Academy boys are at headquarters crying their eyes out."

The director settled back into the comfortable

chair and smiled into the phone. "Yes the Academy boys made it back. They are limping and accusing you of attacking and abandoning them." The Director was fishing.

"I left them to do their job. The short fat one nearly got himself killed. No telling who else would've been hit if the shooting had started. They gave Pots and the Swann brothers a free walk anyway. They are as good as free right now."

"What do you mean the bootleggers are going to walk?" The Director was suddenly at attention and agitated.

"Pots had barely walked into the still when your boy jumped him. They touched no part of the still. It's against the law to make whiskey but it's not against the law to walk in the woods. That is all we have them on. We brought them in on suspicion so they could think about it and spend some money on bail bondsmen and lawyers. We'll never get an indictment." Dave paused.

"Why can't we get an indictment? What is going on down there?" The Director demanded.

"We can't get an indictment because that gung ho Academy fellow you sent down here was in a hurry to yell Internal Revenue Service. He thought he'd get credit for the bust if he hollered first. If he'd waited a minute longer one of them would have touched some part of the still." Dave's grip tightened on the phone. "He nearly got himself shot and maybe some of us along with him. Of course if I'd let Pots shoot him we might have brought some charges against Pots we could make stick."

"I thought you needed the help and they needed the experience. You boys have stopped the flow of whiskey across the river. And that says a lot for your efforts. What is going on there anyway? I have one of the Academy boys wanting to quit and another one, with a fat lip, trying to file charges against you. Neither Harold nor Chester will tell me what happened. What kind of a Keystone Kop's operation do you have going on there?"

"We have a Keystone Kop's operation that is coming to an abrupt halt if you ever try to foist another person into my operation when I've asked you not to." Dave blew up. "You can have my damned badge right now if you want it! I've been weighing the possibility of turning it in anyway!"

"Now don't get your tail feathers ruffled up. Like I say you have stopped the flow of whiskey across the river and took the Governor off my back." The Director realized Dave was serious.

"No, we haven't stopped the flow of whiskey across the river. We've temporarily interrupted it. If we quit today it would start back tomorrow. If we keep the pressure on we can stop it. Now I'm serious about considering turning my badge in."

"You keep the badge." The Director was wise enough to hang up and postpone this kind of talk.

It was Memorial Day, dinner on the ground. Memorial Day is a day of the year all the hill folks congregate in one place. Everyone goes to the cemetery. They care for every grave in that Cemetery as well as the graves of their own people. Most of the folk are related to two thirds of the people who occupy the graves anyway.

Memorial Day is skill day for the women. This

is a place where they can strut their stuff and show what they can do. They dress in the fanciest bonnet and apron they are talented enough to make. The girls and women hand make the flowers used to decorate the graves.

There is an undeclared contest as to which woman is the best cook. It is the women's chance to soar over the treetops or crash and burn in disaster. This meal will be the subject of a whole year's discussion. Each dish will be examined many times during the coming year, recipes exchanged and plans laid for next year. Food of all descriptions; deer, turkey, other kinds of meat, main dishes, cobblers, pies and cakes carefully sat to exhibit their best quality.

The women spread tablecloths on the ground end to end along the fence. These tablecloths cover many feet. Each tablecloth is covered with the best and widest variety of food the woman is capable of producing. Twice as much food as can be ate decorates these cloths. It is a time for men to puff their chest and brag on the food Esmeralda brought.

Decoration Day is a time for children especially

boys. Sweets of this kind are rare in the hills. Decoration Day supplies pies, cakes, cobblers and donuts to spare. The youngsters help the adults with the work but when the lunch triangle rang at noon there never was a child late for the meal.

After meal time the kids are allowed to be kids. The younger girls gather into a knot to giggle and twitter. The older boys walk off down the road to find out who can throw a rock the farthest or the straightest. Of course the older girls are always very interested in these rock throwing contests.

Even though it is a day when they care for and mourn the dead. It is a day the living celebrate being alive. It is a day to associate with friends and other residents of the valley.

Dave was hard at work before anyone arrived. More and more people entered the graveyard. Some would recognize Dave and speak to him. Some worked with him but did not talk to him. Others shunned him altogether. Pots' crowd were the leaders of this group. They couldn't understand how Dave had the nerve to attend but they left him strictly alone.

Dave was aware of her presence when Lesa joined the women decorating the graves. He was also aware of Vera Lee's arrival. He straightened to find her looking at him. When their eyes met she smiled. With a curt nod Dave attacked the weeds he was cutting with a will.

During lunch Lesa openly flirted with Dave and Vera Lee fumed but when Dave looked at Vera Lee she had a smile on her face. Dave went to the black car and retrieved another five gallon jug of water. When he picked the jug up and turned Vera Lee was waiting for him.

"Dave I'm so sorry. I've been such a silly pill." Vera Lee groped for the words. After all the hours of rehearsing she had trouble finding the expression she wished to put forth.

Dave was silent.

"I was just trying to do what Daddy wanted but I learned what Daddy wants and what I want are two different things." Vera Lee was on firmer ground now. She was growing more confident. She knew she had to do it now because her access to Dave was so limited. "I want things to be like they were when we graduated from High School. I want to go to bed with a vision of your face before me at night and wake up with it in the morning."

Dave sat the jug down and took his time doing it. "Do you see this badge on my shirt?"

"Of course I do."

"You told me you'd never have anything to do with me as long as I wore it." Dave looked over her head.

"Well yes, but I was a foolish child then and …"

"I'll be back in minute." Dave waved at Harold who swung into the parking area and leaned on the open door surveying the crowd. He was trying to locate Dave. When Dave waved Harold motioned him to the car.

Vera Lee leaned against the black car and reminded herself to not show how irritated she was at this interruption. After a short conference Harold drove away and Dave returned. He had a look of consternation on his face.

"Dave I want … "

He took her by the shoulders, silencing her again. "Vera Lee there is just no easy way to tell you this so I'll have to just out and tell you." Dave struggled for words. "The Kansas State Highway Patrol arrested a Jason Marley with seven hundred and fifty-five gallons of moonshine whiskey. It has to be your dad."

Vera lee was shocked to silence.

"He took over George Colman's customers. I know it's no consolation to you but they got the whole bunch. They …," Dave broke it off and ducked.

"You son-of-a-bitch!" Vera Lee screamed and swung at him. The blow bounced ineffectively off the side of Dave's head. "Arrest my Dad!" She went after his eyes. He caught her hands.

"I had nothing to do with it. The Kansas State Highway Patrol arrested him." Dave tried to explain.

"You set him up! It's your fault!" She kicked him in the shins.

Mr. Harper led the charging group of people

coming to the commotion. He wrapped his arms around the screaming Vera Lee and looked questioningly at Dave.

"The Kansas State Highway Patrol caught Mr. Marley with a load of whiskey." Dave explained. There was a ripple of voices while the word passed through the crowd then dead silence except for the screaming and sobbing Vera Lee. Everyone looked at her silent Mother. Mother's face was set. There were no tears.

Pots looked at Dave. Now would be a good time to take him. Jason Marley was a well liked member of this community. Most of the people present felt Dave had something to do with Marley's arrest, even though Dave had worked at the cemetery all day. He was a Revenoor! Pots remembered the sledge hammer blows of the last fight and decided not to try it again. *It's too bad I wasn't given more time to set this up* he thought. *None of this crowd would interfere or testify against me.* Pots walked away shaking his head. Another missed opportunity.

Dave leaned against the black car while the

crowd left. Some glared at him forcefully. Others simply ignored him. None gave the standard hill-billy parting words, "Ya'll come and see us now, ye hear?"

Lesa leaned against the car. "I'm sorry," she said softly.

"Me too, I'm not so sorry because of Vera Lee. That torch burned out when I went to college. We just didn't know it yet. We're both trying to reach back for a person who never existed outside our imagination. I'm sorry for her as a daughter with her daddy in trouble, but I'm sorrier for Mr. Marley. I spent a lot of time at his house and in the field with him. I genuinely like and respect the man. There is nothing I can do for him. They got him in Kansas, along with so many others, and with so many gallons of whiskey." Dave was silent for a moment. "What are you doing here? Don't you know they might fire you for consorting with the enemy?"

"Yes, but I live by my judgment. I don't live by anyone else's. I'm not worried about it. If they fire me I'll move on to bigger and better things."

"Like driving a race car?" Dave watched her out of the corner of his eye.

"I won't drive one anywhere but on the track." Lesa turned facing him. "The traffic has grown too fast on the open roads."

"We come out of that one pretty good." Pots sat on a rock facing the Swann brothers. "We beat the charge and kept our still."

"We just dumb lucked out. Miloy had us dead to rights on that one. If that fancy suited little fellow hadn't jumped out early we'd be sitting in jail right now." Joe Joe sat on a log flicking twigs in the creek to watch the little fish flash up and hit them in a swirling splash. The sun was trying climb higher than the trees in the east. The Goggle Eye and the Red Bellied perch were competing for whatever food fell into the cool spring fed pool of water.

"I don't understand why they didn't chop the still up. I've never heard of one they didn't destroy. Do you suppose Miloy is playing with us? He knew they weren't going to make that bust stick so he left us the still so he could catch us again?" Jay Jay eyed the woods suspiciously.

"Naw, that son-without-a-father isn't that smart. I saw him down the hill after we got back. Maybe he thought we had another still down there and was looking for it. I almost got a shot at him. They were just lazy. That's why they didn't chop the still. They were too lazy to move the horses. Good thing I went back up there." Pots took a pull on the jar between him and Joe Joe.

"They have just about got us chocked out. We can't get anything across the river. Marley showed us we can't go north. I don't know about you boys but I'm about broke. We have to sell enough to the local bootleggers to stay alive until we kill Maloy and get back in business." Pots jumped off the rock and paced back and forth restlessly.

"I'm like Lesa; I don't think it's a good idea to kill Miloy. It will just make matters worse. And probably get us hung." This kind of talk was getting Joe Joe restless.

"I think the Feds would swarm in for a few days and then go about their business when they couldn't find anything. It's Miloy that's keeping them on us. Did we ever have this problem before? You know they would come in for awhile then go away. Miloy is keeping them here. What about you Joe Jay?" Pots faced Joe Jay and waited.

Joe Jay looked at his fingers then his toes. His eyes rose to Joe Joe. "Pots, I think you're right. We never had the feds come and stay before now. Miloy has even bought a house and cattle. He ain't planning on going anywhere soon." Joe Jay looked at Joe Joe, "I'll help you burn him out and kill the cattle but I want no part of killing him. That might be a mistake. Some of the people are beginning to like him. I heard George Colman say he is what this country needs."

"Pshaw! Pots snorted. "I used to think George was an all right guy. He ain't nothing but a sneaking coward. No I don't think burning Miloy's place and killing his cows will work. He has to be put out of action quick."

"They know who is operating the still now. They will be watching us. How can we run enough to supply even the local bootleggers?" Joe Joe wanted the subject changed.

"We will run smaller lots and we'll run them at night. We won't go back to the mountains. We will keep the still right here in the valley. We'll make it right under their noses while they look for us in the mountains." Pots wanted them to know he'd put some thought into this. "No one leaves home until after dark and we don't make on moonlight nights."

"They will see our fire." Joe Joe was weighing the possibilities.

"Naw, I've built a pipe thing, like a stove, that will shield the light."

CHAPTER 15

"Have you heard about the dance tomorrow night?" Harold asked Dave.

"You mean the one at Johnson's?" Dave Nodded.

"Are we going?" Chester was interested.

Dave thought about it for a minute and began to chuckle. The chuckle grew into a roaring laugh. He could see people pouring out of the doors and windows at the dance when the Revenoors showed up, every one of them running for the brush with a jar in their hand.

"I hear there is always a lot of moonshine at the dances." Harold was trying to figure out what Dave found so funny.

"I guarantee you there will be a lot of booze there and a lot of people will be drinking it. We've not had much luck getting Judge Webster to do anything with the drinkers. He slaps their hands and sends them home. We're gaining a little with the people of the valley. If we raid that dance we're back to square one."

"I saw Charlie Winters on the road today. I'll bet he goes to the dance." Chester suggested.

"You wouldn't find enough whiskey on Charlie to convict him. It would be too dangerous to try to arrest Charlie in front of that many people. He'd most likely be drinking pretty heavily and someone would be bound to get hurt. Let's get enough on Charlie to convict him."

When the Hill People decide to have a dance it is always held at someone's house. The only municipal buildings in the valley were the schools and churches. Of course these buildings were off limits to drinking bashes like the country dances. No formal invitations were sent out. Word passed down the line announcing the impending dance at the

Johnson's or whoever. Everyone in the valley was automatically invited. These were all night affairs, sometime longer.

Moonshine whiskey flowed like water. At one dance a ten gallon keg of "shine" was introduced at the beginning of the dance. Before the night was over the celebrants were on their way for more whiskey.

At most dances, People brought jugs of whiskey and put them the table. When anyone wanted a drink they served themselves. There was no charge for drinks. It would be a grave breech of etiquette to ask anyone to pay for a drink, perhaps enough of an insult to turn it into a killing offence.

There was very little if any Beer. At some dances there might be a keg of Choctaw Beer. Choctaw Beer has no resemblance to Coors or Bud. It takes an iron constitution to get past the smell and survive a drink of Choctaw Beer.

The music was furnished by local musicians. No formal band existed. These musicians played together all their lives. At this time: Jim picked the lead Guitar, Willis played Rhythm Guitar, Tom worked on the Steel Guitar, Lester and/or Earl took care of the fiddle, Bill played the Mandolin and any other musician who happened to be around joined in.

As you can imagine there were a lot drunk people at these whingdings. A fight always developed. At times no one was fighting anyone in particular. Just hit the person closest to you. Usually a fight between two or more of these hill people was a serious, bloody affair. Somebody got cut, shot or stomped to death. Of course kinfolk of the decedent didn't take kindly to that so the battle continued for sometime. Mostly they were more sensible about the fights that occurred at the dances. They called the dance fight a "whiskey fight " The combatants would come together the next day, have another drink, and laugh about the shenagans of the night before.

No law interfered with these fights. If anyone called the Sheriff he wouldn't come for two or three days. The Sheriff and his Deputies were unpopular beings in the hills and there were people who didn't mind "going a round with them". The law stayed out of the valley all it could.

A division of Marines couldn't stop a dance fight. They could join in the fighting but they couldn't stop it. If a Division of Marines showed up, the Hill People would quit fighting each other and unite against the Marines.

If someone got shot or otherwise killed in the Valley and the Sheriff was called he would come up two or three days later. He waited until combatants sobered up and the shooting stopped. When I say fights I mean fights; fist, feet, teeth, knuckle and skull fights, not arguments. Split lips, broken jaws, missing teeth, split cheeks, and closed eyes were the order of the day.

When the fights started Jim would always say "let's give them music to fight by". Most of the musicians stayed inside and played until the fight was over. There were always a few old guys who came up and sat with the musicians. Nobody molested these men because they wouldn't fight. These men would shoot anyone who bothered him.

The fight at this dance was stopped cold. The people who were outside when the fight began in the house stayed outside. The screen door flew open so hard it came off its hinges. A man landed on his hands and knees on the porch and came up spinning his wheels running for the yard gate. People began pouring out every door, window and any other place they could get out of the house. Some outside people were dumb enough to run up to the windows in order to see why everyone was leaving so fast. Charlie Winters, a very tough, mean old man who lived way back in the mountains and bootlegged whiskey attended this dance. Charlie stood in the middle of the room holding a Colt .45 with the hammer back. Blood formed a slow trickle from his nose and dripped off his chin. He slowly turned around trying to locate the person who hit him.

The next morning a rising sun tossed its fiery fingers across the sky. Charlie squinted into the glare. He was still somewhat hung over from the dance and his nose was a swollen red blob. Charlie's old truck rattled and shuddered its way up beside the gas pump at Harper's store. The gas pump was a true antique. It was quite tall with a long handle attached to the pump. A large glass tube adorned the top. This tube is marked in gallon increments. Up to ten gallon of gas can be pumped, measured and gravity fed into a vehicle.

Charlie Winters climbed stiffly out of the cab and vigorously pumped ten gallon of gas into the glass tank and let it run into the truck. Reaching into the back of the truck he picked up a gallon jar and entered the store.

"Well, dog my cats!" Mr. Harper's feet swung to the floor. "Charlie what brings you out of the hills?"

"I had to come out and I decided to deliver you a jug and chew the fat with you for awhile."

"You know them Revenoors are really getting rough here in the valley. I think I'll pass on the jar for now." Mr. Harper waited for Charlie's reaction.

Charlie reddened, shook the jar and watched the whiskey bead up in it. "I make good whiskey." He growled.

"I know that. I've bought it from you for years.

It's just them Revenoors are tearing the country up right now. I'm not going to keep any whiskey here until things ease up and settle down." Mr. Harper was apologetic but firm.

"Them Revnoors came to my place and I ran them off. I won't stand for any of that nonsense." Charlie glared.

"I'm sorry I can't take it this time."

Charlie turned, slammed through the screen door and stopped. Dave was leaning both forearms on Charlie's truck bed. He was looking at the case of jars resting there.

Neither moved for a long moment, "Charlie we can do this the easy way or one or both of us can die right here."

Charlie's hand moved closer to one of the half dozen guns he was carrying.

"Now Charlie you can't win. All you can do is lose. If you shoot me they'll send an army and dig you out of your cabin on the hill." Dave remained leaning calmly on the edge of the truck bed.

Charlie shifted in the direction of the edge of

the porch.

"I can out run you Charlie and even if you managed to dispose of the jar in your hands there are jars in the box here." Dave spoke calmly, still leaning on the truck.

He made no move. "If you come quietly it will be for a short time. The other way is forever."

"If I come peaceable?" Charlie was on razor edge, very brittle, he could go either way.

"If you come peaceable I'll put a word in with the Judge."

"If I come peaceable," Charlie repeated himself. "Can I wait and come in on my own tomorrow?"

Dave spit on the ground beside the truck and thought about the proposition. It was far from protocol and farther from his wishes but anything was better than a shoot out with this tough old man. He knew if Charlie gave his word he would honor it to the letter.

"Ok, if you leave that jug sitting on the porch and I take all this in the pickup. You lay all the guns you are wearing beside the jar on the porch." Dave doubted Charlie would give up the guns.

"My guns? No way I'm going to let you have them. Why if I gave you my guns you might not keep your word." Charlie tensed up again.

"Charlie how long have you known me?" Dave remained so casual and calm Charlie was having trouble believing this was a life and death situation.

"I've known you all your life. That is the reason I haven't already shot you dead. Dave, you used to buy a drink from me in the old days."

"Did you ever know of me not keeping my word? It's only because I've known and respected you all these years we are standing here talking. Otherwise we'd have taken you down hard and let the chips fall where they may." Dave shifted to a more alert position. "What's it going to be Charlie?"

Charlie glared but he slowly eased the jar to the porch. Dave had an uneasy moment when Charlie's hand disappeared under his shirt. The hand came out slowly and placed a revolver beside the jug. Carefully Charlie gathered all six guns scattered from his neck to his boots and lay them carefully on them on the porch.

Dave breathed a sigh of relief. His hand slipped down and snapped the safety on the pistol stuck under his belt at the front of his shirt. He lifted the box of jars from the pickup and sat them on the ground. Charlie tromped around to the driver's door.

"I'll see you tomorrow?" Dave asked pointedly.

"Yes," Charlie grunted and drove away.

The screen door spring sang and Mr. Harper stepped out looking after Charlie with his hands on his hips. "I'd never have believed it could happen. I thought Charlie would die before he was arrested. And I can't believe you let him come to town tomorrow."

"He'll be there. Charlie's word is good." Dave was feeling let down after the adrenaline died.

"Of course Charlie's word is good. Do you think you can have an influence with the Judge?"

"Charlie will get three or four years for this." Dave nodded to the whiskey. "I'm going to talk myself blue in the face to get the Judge to make it all probation."

"You know Charlie is going to make whiskey again." Mr. Harper was trying to understand all that was happening here.

"Sure he will. I'm hoping he will limit it to himself and perhaps a close friend or two. If not I'll have to arrest him again for parole violation."

The director was livid. "What do you mean, he will be in tomorrow? You have the whiskey? You caught him red-handed and he'll be in tomorrow?" The Director was more than a little bit upset.

"Old Charlie is a curly wolf from way back in the hills. It was the only way I could take him without a shoot out. As it was, I took six handguns off him and I could see several long guns in the cab of the pickup." Dave said.

"Shoot out? You're a Federal Officer; he wouldn't dare shoot an Internal Revenue Agent. We'd send an army after him." The Director was indignant.

"Like I told you Charlie is a curly wolf from way back in the hills. He would fire on a battalion of Marines if they riled him. He might whip the Marines if he was on his home range. Charlie is the type that will soak up several hits and keep shooting until he dies. If I'd had that surly, ambitious Academy man with me the three of us would be dead. To these people waving a badge is a hostile act. To a lot of the old timers it is a declaration of war." Dave was hoping to get the fact known that these people had a different notion of law and order than their city counter parts.

"These people moved into the mountains years ago to be left alone. They elect their Sheriffs with the tacit understanding he stay on flat land and leave them alone. The only laws they recognize are the ones they make among themselves. There is not one lawsuit going on between these people. If there is a problem they settle it between themselves.

"Now we are not only telling them they have to obey our law. We're taking a very substantial part of their livelihood away and worse yet sending part of the population to prison. These people traditionally band together in times of trouble. Most are related to each other. That is the reason you could make no headway until now. If we do something bad we'll have people who neither make nor drink whiskey sitting alongside the road with a rifle waiting for a Revnoor to shoot at. Remember the British Army's trip home from Lexington and Concord? You send an army in here after Charlie and you better have it well armed because it might face a revolution." Dave paused. "It was the best deal we could make with Charlie."

"The academy man I sent out there quit the force when I refused to discipline you and give him credit for the arrest. I told him it was a bad bust but he wanted it anyway." The Director came as close to apologizing as he ever would. "You're making headway. We'll do it your way. We're getting some contacts now. The last one told us whiskey was being bootlegged out of the Cripple Creek Store."

"That's Jack LaRue. We have already marked him for a raid. He's a Pots, Swann customer and we're going to take him out in order to strangle those boys some more. They have to be hurting financially. They will make a mistake soon."

At 8 AM Dave eased the agency pickup truck up

alongside Charlie's truck and motioned Charlie to follow him into the Court House. Two hours later, having been booked and bailed out, Charlie was on his way back to the hills. He stopped at a pawn shop two blocks from the Court House and picked up several handguns.

Later, the same day, Dave, Chester and Harold wheeled into the Cripple Creek store. The store sat about a hundred yards back from the unpaved county road. Jack located the store back from the road in order to avoid some of the dust.

A small meadow lay across the driveway. Giant red oak trees surrounded the store and a post oak grew at each corner of the house. These trees were probably three hundred years old. A massive sycamore cast its shade on the corner of the meadow. Scattered under the sycamore tree were some benches and a table.

The benches and table were an informal meeting place for the people of the community. It was a place where people exchanged news and visited with one another. The senior people of the community often met to play checkers or dominos.

Every man there carried a knife as sharp as a straight razor and he'd carried this knife since he was chin high to a grasshopper. A large number of these men chewed tobacco or dipped snuff. While they passed the time of day most would whittle things out of wood. They made buzzers, tops, sling shots and other toys for the kids. They also whittled boat paddles, containers, and other useful things. The skill of the men with a knife is unbelievable. It was inevitable the benches be called the spit and whittle benches.

Dave handed Jack a copy of the search warrant and turned to face three horsemen cutting across the meadow. "Tell them you are closed." Dave instructed Jack.

"Hell no!" Jack erupted. "That warrant may give you the right to search my place but it doesn't give you the right to run any of my customers off."

"It might be less embarrassing when we find your stash." Dave didn't want a gallery watching the search.

"You aren't going to find anything." Jack was losing his temper. "I may need witnesses to what you boys do here. You may try to plant a jug on me."

"You tell them to stay out of the store until we are through."

The onlookers took a seat on the spit and whittle benches and began a good natured bantering. Hurrahing they called it.

The Agents went over the store with a fine toothed comb. They checked every inch of the floor and counters. They dumped the barrel of Pinto beans. They went under the store.

"If you find a Copperhead or big Rattler under there bring him out with you." One of the spit and whittle crowd yelled derisively.

Dave eyed a ladder leaning against the store. "Do you suppose there is a trap door in the roof?"

"We'll find out." Harold scooted up the ladder. After a close inspection he climbed dejectedly down.

As they were finishing the store a pickup truck drove up and five men joined the group at the spit and whittle bench. Dave led the searchers to the house. When they left the store the onlookers erupted with yells, whistles and cat calls.

"If we find anything I'm going to arrest the whole bunch." Harold grouched.

"You couldn't make it stick." Dave was concerned.

"If we find any illegal whiskey I can arrest them for being on the premises with illegal alcoholic beverages. They would have to post bail to get out of jail." Harold growled.

"It would be thrown out at arraignment. Look at the rifle leaning against every knee out there. Do you realize how quickly this could turn ugly? If anyone arrests them I think I will let you do it. Besides, they are laughing and in a good mood. If you go out and arrest them we'll lose all the good will we've worked so hard to develop." Dave patted Harold on the shoulder. "We're going to have a lot of spectators before this is over."

"How do you know we're going to get more spectators?"

"See those that just came in? Look at those coming up the road. The backwoods telegraph is running full speed and everyone will come to see what we find. Wave at them, laugh and joke with them." Dave advised. He wanted to get this done quickly yet thoroughly.

A through search of the house yielded nothing except more cheering, cat calls and whistles from the growing crowd around the benches.

A search of the barn and out building was as unproductive as the rest. They rigged a boson's chair and lowered Chester in the well. Still nothing.

"We know he has it. But we're not going to find it let's go." Dave said.

The crowd increased steadily. Cat calls were long and loud when they reached the top of the hill behind the store.

Jack watched the caravan disappear over the hill and raised his hands over his head and yelled, "This calls for a drink!" Leading the way to a misshapen, rained soaked old paper box lying in the county road ditch he pulled out a gallon jar and passed it around.

One of the crowd handed money to Jack. "I want a half gallon." He said.

Jack thought for a moment. "You know where Smith's road turns off the county road? There is an old lightning blasted snag just past the corner. You should look at it on your way home."

"I want a gallon." Another man had money in his hand.

"You know where Iron Springs Trail is? Well look behind the big rock on the left hand side of the trail.

It was a disgusted Dave who reported to the Director. "We know Jack LaRue had the whiskey. We just couldn't find it. I don't think he had any at the store. Maybe we got there just after he sold the last jar of it. Right now he's Pots biggest customer." Dave explained to the Director.

"Well you boys missed him. I have a couple of the Academy boys here."

Dave sucked in a breath and spun angrily raising a finger.

"Now hold on. Hold up a minute and let's talk about it. I have these Academy boys and I have to assign them somewhere. I have them working in every district except yours. The Dean of the Academy is biting me because two are still unassigned. He will be going to the Governor if I don't get them assigned soon." The Director reached out and pushed Dave's finger down. "Holster that thing and hear me out."

Dave frowned but held his peace.

"I'm going to send the Academy boys after Jack LaRue. None of you will have to work with them. It would be nice if you gave them a word of advice occasionally." The Director paused to gauge the effect his words were having on the three Agents. "They understand that all three of you are senior and are their boss. You will not have to work with them. Come on fellows I need help here."

"They won't be on our case or get in our way?" Dave was skeptical.

"That's right. I'll assign them to Jack LaRue and order them to stay clear of or check with you on

BATTLE OF WHISKEY VALLEY

anything else."

"Ok," Dave surrendered. "But they're to understand they do not interfere with the Pots, Swann
case in any manner."

Dave set Agents Henry and Clyde up on Buckhorn Mountain. With the use of a high powered
telescope they could see into the Cripple Creek
Store.

"From here you can see what is going on down
at the store. If you see LaRue get a delivery of moonshine you are not to interfere. Now hear me! You
are not to interfere with a delivery if it happens under your noses." Dave was emphatic.

"These woods are full of hunters, fishermen and
people tending their livestock. Don't build a fire,
smoke or talk while you are here. If you do they will
find you. Leave the reflector suppressor on the end
of that telescope at all times. If the sun reflects off
the lens it can be seen for miles."

Three weeks later Henry fidgeted, "Clyde, will
you relieve me on the scope?" he whispered. They'd
sat behind the scope for three weeks. They'd seen

a lot of people come and go but they had not seen any kind of whiskey changing hands or otherwise.

Clyde settled behind the scope and took a half hearted glance through the scope. Leaping to attention he fastened his eye to the scope. "LaRue has company," he announced.

Henry leaped to his feet and tried to focus the binoculars on the Cripple Creek Store. The distance was too great to pickup small details but there were a group of horses entering the meadow in front of the store. Pots was riding the lead horse. Full burlap bags were tied together at the top and hung on either side of the horses he was leading.

Jack looked at the load the horses were carrying. "That looks like more than I ordered."

"There are a few extra jars but we figured you could sell it. We ran a little extra." Pots stepped off the horse and stretched.

"Did you know Miloy and his boys were here?" Jack was scratching his head and looking at the sacks. Greed nibbled at him. "With Miloy and his boys on a rampage it's hard to sell a jar these days.

I'd have to have a price break on that many jars."

"We figured you could sell this many." Pots twisted his hat brim and held onto his temper. "We can't sell it for less. We're not making anything as it is."

"Tell you what. I can't pay for that much right now but if you want to leave it I'll pay for it as I sell it." Jack was going to find some angle on this deal.

Pots twisted his hat and held on. They needed money too bad not to take the deal. He was sure the Swann brothers would understand. "Ok but are you smart enough to know what will happen if you get cute with us?"

"Yeah, let's unload this into the pickup before someone comes along. Them Revnoor got me jumpy."

It was with great interest Henry and Clyde watched the jars being stacked neatly in the pickup bed. They began picking up things around their lookout.

"It's too late to do anything today. Miloy left strict instructions not to molest a delivery to LaRue. We'll get LaRue in the morning we know he has the stuff on the premises." Henry was thinking this would be his first bust.

"Do you think we should notify Miloy and company of the coming bust or not?" Clyde was trying to figure out what could go wrong.

"No, we were assigned to LaRue. He is our worry alone. Although I want to see Miloy's face when he finds out we did it."

The sky was getting gray in the east. Dawn was on its way. The Academy boys were sitting on the hill overlooking the Cripple Creek Store. They were not going be late for their first bust. A tinge of color rose in the east. Cranking the engine Clyde drove off the hill.

Before they reached the bottom of the hill Jack's old Ford F-100 turned in their direction. He was close enough Henry had to scramble to get the Red light on top of the agency car.

Jack stopped and reached for something in the seat on his right.

Henry ran to the truck window just in time to grab a quart jar Jack was attempting to dump out the window. Jack knew that if he broke the jar it could be used against him in a court of law. If he dumped the contents there was no evidence against him. Some of the whiskey spilled but Henry managed to save a little over a pint. Holding the jar aloft he looked at the pickup bed. It was empty! There was nothing back there! Clyde dashed down the right side of the F-100. He was stunned. "Oh, no."

"Where is the whiskey?" Henry demanded.

"You have it in your Hand." Jack pointed out.

"I'm not talking about this piddling amount. Where is the stuff you bootleg out of the Store?" Henry looked at him accusingly. "We're going to find it. With what we have and we seen you come out of the store parking lot. We don't need a search warrant."

"Miloy and his boys went over this place with a fine toothed comb a little while ago. They didn't find anything."

"Maybe we search better than Miloy. They taught us how to search at the Academy. And seeing as how we found this whiskey on you we don't need a search warrant." Henry was sure the whiskey was there. He saw them unload it last evening just at dark.

"Well you boys search all you want to. I'll even give you permission to search. I'm definitely in no hurry to go to town with you all." Jack leaned back in the seat and pulled his hat over his eyes.

Three hours later a dejected pair of Agents returned to the car. "Where did you put that whiskey?" Clyde asked.

"In the seat of my pickup, right where you found it. Speaking of whiskey I'd appreciate it if you boys would have me in a cell in the next few minutes. I'm going into withdrawals." Jack's face screwed up and a shudder shook his frame.

"It ain't been that long since you had a drink." Henry pointed out

"It don't take me long to go into them." Jack held a quivering hand out. "I want you to promise me you won't hurt me." Jack's voice shook.

"Hurt you? Why would we want to hurt you?" Clyde mopped his brow and took a pull at his water bottle.

"Well when I get into a good withdrawal I go crazy. They tell me I yell, bite, cuss and try to attack everyone near me. I know I wet and soil my clothes and vomit. Of course if you use a little Pine Sol it will make the clean up easier."

"Not in my car you don't." Clyde warned. "I'm not going around with that smell in my car."

"There's a very simple way to prevent it. Just give me a sip out of the jar." Jack shuddered again.

"We can't give you a sip out of that jar. It's evidence." Henry was shocked.

"Ok. There is a bunch of it and a little smidgen wouldn't be missed. You would still have your evidence." Jack humped up into a quivering ball on the seat.

Henry rolled the jar around in his hands. "You know he's right. We don't need it all for a conviction. My stomach isn't strong enough to ride to town in a smelly car."

Clyde took the lid off the jar and held it up to Jack's lips. Jack sipped as much as Clyde would let him.

"AAAH," Jack said. "That is good whiskey. You boys should taste it."

"We told you it was evidence."

"This is straight off the worm. It hasn't been cut. There is no water in this. If you guys are going to work at this job you should know what good whiskey is. There is plenty in the jar for evidence. Aw come on, a taste isn't going to hurt you."

"After all that searching I could use a little drink." Clyde held the jar up and eyed the whiskey level in it. "It could stand to have a couple of drinks taken out of it." Taking a drink out of the jar he handed it to Henry who followed suit.

"That is good whiskey. Who made it?" Henry fished. Jack was silent.

The car ran down the hill, crossed the spring branch, and started up the steep incline of the next hill. "This is whiskey Hill." Jack said from the back seat. "All the local people stop here for a drink. I'm feeling a little shaky again."

Henry looked over the seat back at him.

"Is it true that I'm the first bust you guys have

made?" Jack questioned.

Clyde grunted assent.

"Ain't that something? Here you guys are just getting out of the Academy and you do something Miloy and company couldn't do."

"What are you talking about?" Henry was curious.

"Well Miloy and his boys come over and stayed all day and when they left old Jack was still at home. It didn't take you boys long to round old Jack up. Wheel in here and let's have a drink to celebrate your good work."

After a couple more celebrations on the way to town the level in the jar was getting alarmingly low. Everyone was feeling mellow. Henry left the jar within Jack's reach. Clyde and Henry were discussing what they would do when they replaced Miloy. Jack quietly screwed the lid off the jar. Snatching the jar he drank in long swallows. Henry jerked the jar away from Jack. Eyeing the level in the jar he began to cuss.

Clyde looked at the Jar. "That's alright. Most

of this moonshine has been watered down anyway. We'll put some water in the jar before arraignment hearing tomorrow morning.

The next morning it came Jack's turn to stand before the Judge. "You have been charged with being in possession of an alcoholic beverage on which no taxes were paid. How do you plead?"

"Not guilty your honor."

"Your honor the defendant was arrested when IRS Agents found this jar of illegal whiskey in a pickup truck registered to and driven by the defendant." The District Attorney indicated the offending jar on his desk. "Your honor that isn't moonshine whiskey in the jar, it is water."

"Your honor two Internal Revenue Agents arrested the defendant and brought him in. They would hardly have arrested him for having a jar of water."

'This is an interesting situation." The Judge mused. "Bailiff bring the jar to the bench." The judge screwed the lid off and took a drink out of the jar. The Judge's face screwed into a mask and he spit the liquid into a spittoon beside his bench. "Water!" He gasped; shaking his head he wiped his mouth and spat into spittoon again. "Case dismissed!" The gavel came down with a bang.

With a relieved smile Jack walked out of the courtroom. The District Attorney stared at Clyde and Henry.

CHAPTER 16

The sun shined on the tree and left a mottled cool shade on the ground. Pots and the Swann brothers dropped in the shade mopping their brow.

"We need money." Joe Joe declared.

"Don't we all?" Pots agreed.

"We want to know what happened to the money for that last batch of whiskey we ran off for Jack LaRue?" Joe Jay demanded.

"He didn't have the money to pay for it. We have to wait until he sells it." Pots was becoming fully awake.

"I don't stay one step ahead of Miloy and make

this stuff for fun. You pay us and collect from Jack." Joe Joe's voice was firm.

"I'd be happy to pay you but I don't have the money. Honest fellows, Jack will pay. We just have to hang in there." Pots knew these boys from childhood. He knew they were thoroughly agitated.

"Are you sure Jack didn't pay you?" Joe Jay pressed.

The insult stung home. Pots looked for his rifle. It sat against a tree several feet away. "You boys better go ask Jack."

"We intend to ask him and collect for all he got. We're quitting the still business. We don't intend to make any more whiskey." Joe Joe watched Pots closely.

Pots held his hands out. "Fellows I can't give you what I don't have. Go check with Jack and come back and help me run this batch."

"We think we've been short changed and we won't be back." Joe Jay strode to his horse. Joe Joe watched Pots until Joe Jay could take the chore over and mounted his horse.

"All right! Pots shouted. "All right! I can make better whiskey and make more money out of it if I don't carry you lazy blanket butts!" Pots looked at the rifle and knew they would be out of range before he got to it. I'm better off without them he lied to himself but he felt like a huge gulf was opening beneath his feet.

The Swann brothers rode silently. They could also feel the great gulf they'd opened in their friendship with Pots. The horses moved slowly in the hot humid air. Joe Joe pulled up on the ridge overlooking Pots's farm. The men rested in a dark shade. They came to a silent agreement and rode down the hill.

The brothers left the traveled trail and approached Pots's barn through the brush. Each struck a match and tossed the flaming missiles into the hay loft before the Sulfa quit burning on them. They rode a wide circuitous route around to the front of the house and stopped under cover of the bushes. They patiently watched the smoke and fire in the barn grow to huge proportions.

When the family rushed to the fire at the barn Joe Jay handed his reins to Joe Joe and walked into the house. He smashed two kerosene lamps against the wall near the curtains. Tossing a match in the pool of kerosene he walked out. In the excitement of the barn fire no one noticed the house fire until it was too late.

Pots sat contemplating the morning's proceedings. What happened? What made the Swanns so suspicious? He'd collected no money from Jack. Joe Joe and Joe Jay had chugged along loyally in his wake since they were infants. What got under their blankets? It's Miloy's fault. He constantly dogged them, slowly tightened the noose, keeping their nerves raw and frayed. The mention of Miloy put a knot in Pots's stomach and he was a lot stronger than the Swann Brothers. He was sure the Swann Brothers would be back. He'd get the money from Jack and pay them off. He'd even give them part of his share. He could fix it. He dozed off.

He woke and looked around drowsily. He leaped to his feet wide awake when he saw the smoke billow over the valley. He knew, in his gut, what it was. He mounted his horse and brought it off the mountain at a dead run until he came to the spot where the Swann Brothers stopped earlier.

Everything was revealed in stark reality. He jumped from his horse and threw up. Anxiously he counted people around the fires. Everyone was alright. His house, his barn, the winter's food, the food for his livestock, the corn he'd set apart to make whiskey, all gone. He had nothing but some scorched ground. He knew who did it and he knew exactly how they did it.

He cursed the day the Swann brothers were born and leaped on the horse's back. Viciously jerking the horse's head around he drove the spurs home. The horse descended the ridge in long stone rattling strides. At the fork Pots took the trail leading away from his home. He held the scared gelding to a ground eating long lope. Rivers of sweat and then white foam flecks flew from the horse but Pots' spur held him to the pace.

At the edge of the clear space around Joe Joe's

house he pulled the Winchester rifle from its boot and walked his horse in. There didn't appear to be anyone home. He turned his horse to the fancy barn Joe Joe built while times were good and whiskey flowed. He rode down the hall in the center of the barn and noted the stalls were empty.

Pots tied the gelding behind the barn and walked back through the hall to the barn door and scanned the area. He could not see nor hear anyone. He looked the barn over carefully. Yep, old Joe Joe built a nice barn.

Looking the surrounding area over he noted the outhouse sat on a small rise and faced the trail he'd rode in on. He seated himself on the boards of the outhouse seat and pushed the door almost shut, leaving a crack of two inches. He'd barely got seated and checked his rifle when he heard the drum of horse's feet and rumble of voices.

"I'd sure like to see Pots's face when he comes home." Joe Jay chucked.

"That will teach him to cheat us." Joe Joe felt bad about the fires and needed to justify them in his mind.

Pots pulled the hammer back and rested the rifle barrel on the frame of the out house door. Joe Jay, he thought, you are behind this, I'll gut shoot you and listen to you squeal. Aiming carefully so as not hit Joe Jay's backbone he pulled the trigger. The rifle leaped and roared. Pots worked the lever to bring a fresh round into the chamber rapidly. He noted Joe Jay was sliding off his horse head first. Confused, Joe Joe pulled his horse to a stop. The sights settled squarely in center of his chest and the rifle roared once more. The shock of the 170 grain Silvertip bullet going through Joe Joe's medicine bag sent a spray of blood, bone and meat out the backside and drove Joe Joe out of the saddle over the back of his horse.

Both horses bolted. Pots levered another round into the chamber and opened the door. He continued to sit on the outhouse seat. Joe Joe lay absolutely still. Joe Jay writhed in pain.

Pots rose and walked carefully to Joe Jay. He noted the hole in Joe Jay's back. Hooking his toe under Joe Jay's shoulder he flipped him onto his back. The bullet had cut an artery. The blood was pulsing out the hole. He spit in Joe Jay's face.

"Did you enjoy burning my place?" he asked sarcastically.

Joe Jay's lips moved.

"You're going to die a lot faster than I wanted you to." Pots kicked Joe Jay in the side of the head and sat on a log at the edge of the clear space and watched the writhing Joe Jay become an inert lump of clay.

"Why did they burn me out?" He asked himself over and over. The anger was dying in him and the import of the last couple of hours was beginning to hit home. He'd known and liked the Swann Brothers all his life. They'd crawled on the same pallet at the social functions before they could walk. He again looked at the inert forms lying motionless in the dust. A real sense of grief washed over him.

He rose to his feet and held both arms out. "What did you make me do it for?" he shouted the question to the wind.

"Do it for, do it for, do it for?" The mountains laughed at him.

"Miloy!" He screamed. Miloy, Miloy, Miloy the echoes mocked him and the Pines sighed in the wind. If it wasn't for Miloy none of this would have happened. Miloy slowly strangled them. He systematically destroyed their markets and business leaving them on starvation. All the hard work they spent constantly on the move and the hours and days of looking over their shoulders. Miloy was like a Bloodhound. He just kept the pressure on. A lazy whirlwind spun its way slowly across the dusty circle. It ruffled Joe Jay's hair and left a film of dust on the corpses

Pots strode to his horse. Without a backward glance he rode up the ridge. When he reached the still there was still some hot coals left from the morning fire. He gathered all the junky wood he could find and threw it on the fire. He sized the ax and cut green saplings. He threw the saplings on the fire. It began to smoke in a most satisfactory manner.

Dave, Harold and Chester sat around the cold sooty black stove in Harper's store. Each ate a sandwich and drank a soda. The conversation was around the attributes of two fishing streams up the valley. The door spring sang its warning song and George Colman stepped past the screen into the store.

"Pots's house is on fire." He announced on his way to the cold drink case. He pulled an Orange Crush from the case and turned to Harper. "Are you out of ice already?"

"Did you say Pots' house was on fire?" Dave was on his feet. This was an unexpected development.

"House and barn both," George put the drink back in the box. "I stopped by. It was too late. It looked like it got a fast start and Pots's wasn't home. Just the woman and kids."

This was an unexpected development. There was a rattle of paper bags as the Revenoors prepared to leave.

"Who would have the nerve or be stupid enough to burn Pots out?" Dave wondered aloud.

"I'd like to get there and look around before he

gets back." Harold was thinking ahead.

"House and Barn burning and Pots is not home. None of this makes any sense. It may be a setup. We better stay spread out until we ascertain what is happening. Watch Pots's wife and the two oldest boys."

"They are pretty small …" Chester began.

"They've killed and skinned deer half their life." Dave interrupted. "Don't kid yourself. With their up bringing they are both capable and able to kill you"

"You boys better be damned careful around Pots's house." George called through the door as they left.

The road was beautifully dappled with shade from the afternoon sun. The breeze swayed the treetops which gave the shades a life of their own. Dave failed to see any of the beauty.

This isn't right. It does not fit, he thought. *Who would have the nerve or stupidity to burn Pots out in the middle of the day? Who would have the nerve to do it anytime? There were enough people who hated and feared Pots's bullyboy ways but everyone knew burning Pots out would end in a death or a series of deaths.*

One thing you could be sure of, the house and barn were burned simultaneously. It was a clear case of arson. When he topped the last hill Dave saw the smoke billow up on the mountain. What was this? The fire on the mountain should be a whiskey still fire, but whose? Pots and the Swann brothers were too careful to build this sort of fire. The wood they used to make a whiskey run with gave off almost no smoke. What in the heck was happening here?

Dave dragged a billowing cloud of dust into the clearing where Pots house used to stand.

"We'll check the smoke on the mountain. Take your rifles with you," Dave said when they arrived on the scene. "Be very, very careful. None of this makes any sense."

Pots's wife and kids stood in a compact group. Not one of them acknowledged the Revenoor's presence.

The house and barn were already down to embers and smoke. The agents worked their way around the scene of devastation and eased up the ridge. Spread out as they were they could cover one another. At the top of the ridge they looked back down on the smoldering house and barn. Dave still hadn't got a handle on it. Continuing onward, they moved even more slowly and picked their cover more carefully.

There was a huge boulder with a tree down on top of it, Dave decided to use it for cover. He eased in closer and tried to get in sight of the still. Pots rose from behind the boulder like the Devil himself. His Winchester centered on Dave's chest and a broad smile creased his lips.

Dave was late and he knew he was late. Swinging his rifle around he attempted to step sideways. He saw the fire blossom out of the end of Pots's rifle and felt the bullet bite home in his chest. Dave staggered backward and watched Chester's bullet jump the dust from Pots' shirt and Harold's explode Pots's head like a ripe watermelon.

Dave threw up a large amount of bright blood. The starch went out of his knees and collapsed to the ground on his face. The warm blackness rose and welcomed him to total darkness.

Lesa adjusted the long black veil to hide the flow of tears. She had been seated in the first row of seats back from the casket. Her eyes rose over the casket and met Vera Lee's. It was a shock. Vera Lee's mouth was set in a hard thin line. Her eyes hurled daggers across the casket in Lesa's direction. Her brow was wrinkled. No tears stained her eyes. She'd aged ten years since Decoration Day.

But Lesa had to admit Vera Lee looked awfully good in the black dress anyway. Lesa's eyes wandered past the caskets and settled on the third one. How dare they bury Pots on the same day and so near? Lesa's stomach boiled. She had respect For Joe Joe and Joe Jay. For Pots she felt nothing but loathing.

The Swann brothers followed Pots lead all through school and continued on into adulthood. It was Pots who led them down the wrong road into the moonshine business. How could he do it? How could Pots shoot men he'd been lifelong friends with? It was like Pots had shot his brothers.

After the funeral Lesa strolled slowly back to

the parking lot. She was watchful for Vera Lee. She knew a showdown with Vera Lee was inevitable but this was not the time or place. A jury found Jason Marley guilty and sentencing was set for tomorrow. Vera Lee was close to the edge and very brittle.

Vera Lee was going through a terrible metamorphous. Since Marley's arrest her Mother had withdrawn and shrank. Vera Lee lost the two men dearest to her and to some extent her mother also. She was suddenly and violently yanked from a protected, frivolous, plotting school girl into the real world of being the head of a household. It seemed her whole world caved in at once.

"Just a moment," a voice stopped Lesa when she opened the car door. Lesa turned to see Mr. Harper hurry toward her. Even his steps have slowed down she thought.

"How is Dave?" Mr. Harper questioned.

"He's about the same. He's still in a coma. The bullet wrecked his right lung. It missed his spine. If he recovers he will be able to walk. The Doctors say it can still go either way but each day he lives makes his recovery seem more hopeful."

"Dave's lucky to have someone stay and nurse him twenty-four hours a day. If anyone can pull him out of it you can."

The rattle of a window blind pulled Dave's eyes open. He tried to raise his head but the effort was too much. Light streamed through the window and outlined the figure standing in front of it. The figure seemed to glow.

"Are you an Angel?" He croaked.

Lesa's knees went limp. She reached for the window sill to steady herself. "No, I'm not an Angel and don't plan to be one as far as you are concerned."

By the time Lesa reached his side Dave'd lapsed back into sleep. But it seemed like sleep to her, not the coma he'd been in. She settled in the chair beside his bed. A smile lit her lips. Lesa had pulled Dave back from the brink by sheer will power so many times in the past month. Her steady hand and calm voice gave him something to hold onto. It gave him a reason to come back.

Dave's recovery was agonizingly slow. But the fact he'd survived a high powered rifle bullet to the chest was an amazing feat. He'd progressed to the state he could be raised to a sitting position. "I have to get out of here and see to the place. Do I have any cows left?"

"Skinny old Terry Midler has ridden that bony old mule to your place and baby sat your cows everyday. They're in better shape than they were when you were caring for them. He said he owed you a lot more than feeding some cows. The barn you laid out has been built. The members of the community held a barn raising. George Colman cut and baled your hay meadows. The young men of the community hauled the hay and stacked it in your new barn. You've become a full fledged member of this community again." Lesa fluffed Dave's pillow.

Dave reached up and pulled Lesa down and kissed her. "We've become members of this community." He corrected her. When Lesa straightened he placed something in her hand. Opening her hand she saw it was his badge.

"What am I supposed to do with this?" She demanded.

"Give it to the director and tell him I'm getting married and won't need it anymore." Dave smiled at the thought.

"You can't get out of it that easy. The doctors say you will be able to go back to work." Lesa slapped the badge back into his hand. "The man I fell in love with wore one of these things. Don't go changing things on me." Lesa was silent for a moment. "It's supposed to be a secret but as soon as you can stand the Governor is going to pin the State's Metal of Valor on your chest and promote you to Director for this area."